*Swānanda*

Gaṇapati Dēvasthāna

2026.0603

Srinivas Shastri

ॐ *Swānanda*

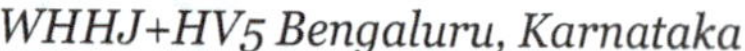

WHHJ+HV5 Bengaluru, Karnataka

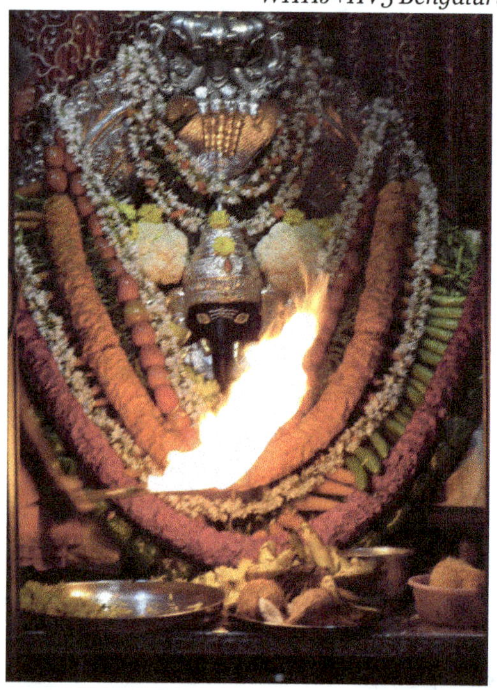

Sri Vinayaka Devasthana, *4th Block, Jayanagar*

Cover Photo by Author at *Swānandāshrama*
Author Photo at home

To All Lovers of Ganesha
and
Mom (1942~2021),
born a couple of days before *Vināyaka Chaviti*

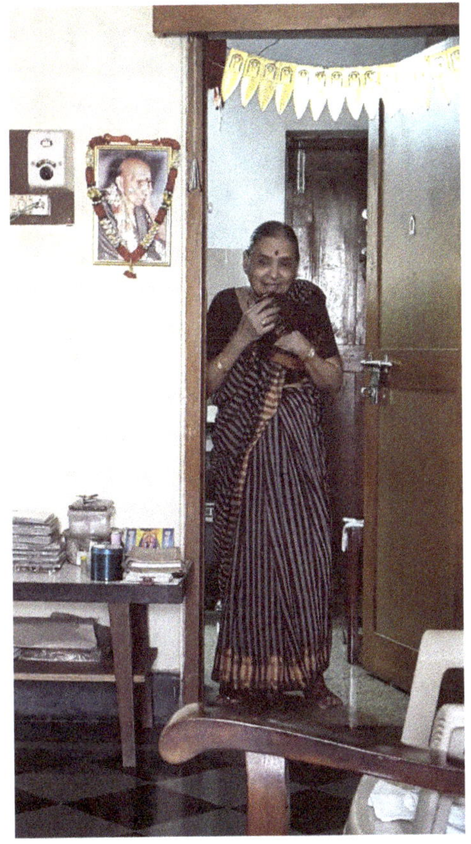

Mom on the Ides of March, 2016

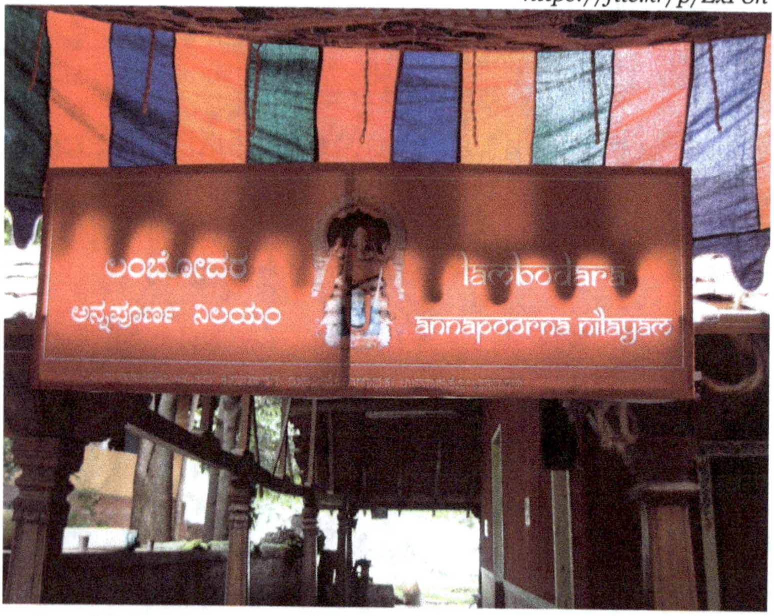

Lambōdara Annapoorna Nilayam at Swānandāshrama,
named after Mom, in June 2007

In Gratitude

With heartfelt thanks to:

- Mal, for communicating the *ādēsh* [command] from Sai Baba of Shirdi, which initiated a series of books
- Santhosh Rāvel, the prime mover behind Swānandāshrama, and his infectious enthusiasm in the compilation of this book; he'll be referred to as Rāvel in this book
- ShivKumar AP, for the Gaṇapati images
- For rendering the *dhyāna śloka* of **all** 32 Gaṇapati:
    - Anuj, in Kannada in his soothing voice; he also reviewed the usage of the same in this book
    - Shobhana Ravishekhar, in Tamil
    - Satwik JOGLEKAR, in Marathi
    - Padmaraj Kumar GUDA, in Telugu
- Sudarśan S, for his enlightening and voluminous feedback
- PSM, for his suggestions
- Karjol and HPR, for their feedback on the usage of Kannada
- My chromeOS devices (LG Chromebase with the Asus Chromebox and HP Chromebook), which made writing this book in Google Docs such a pleasure

None of us
is as good
as all of us
~Ray Kroc

We were the
Lords of All Creation
~Red in Shawshank

Notes

- Gaṇapati, Ganesha, and Vināyaka all refer to the elephant-headed Hindu God
- **Master** refers to Sri Ramakrishna
- **Swami** refers to Sri Satya Sai Baba of "Put-apart-the-i"
- **Boldfacing** in quotes used has been done by the author, unless otherwise specified
- This document uses US spellings and follows the Times of India Edit Page style of using the lower-case **i**, except at the start of sentences. The Big I refers to the Self, in which all things appear and disappear
- All photos/images are shot/made by the author, unless otherwise indicated
- You can use Google Lens to scan links given as QR Codes and translate text in other scripts to your language of choice
- The plural of *Indian words* will be the same word; suffixing them with an **s** seems to be a travesty
- Names from Indian history and mythology might **not** be italicized
- Feel that the period is superfluous at the end of paragraphs

Table of Contents

Gaṇapati Dēvasthāna

Here are the coordinates of Swānandāshrama:

App/Website	**Link / QR Code**
Google Earth	*https://bit.ly/geSwananda* 
Google Maps	*https://maps.app.goo.gl/NCuGt3WWTgCdp3fm7* 
Please use this QR Code to contribute to the Swānandāshrama Gaṇapati Dēvasthāna	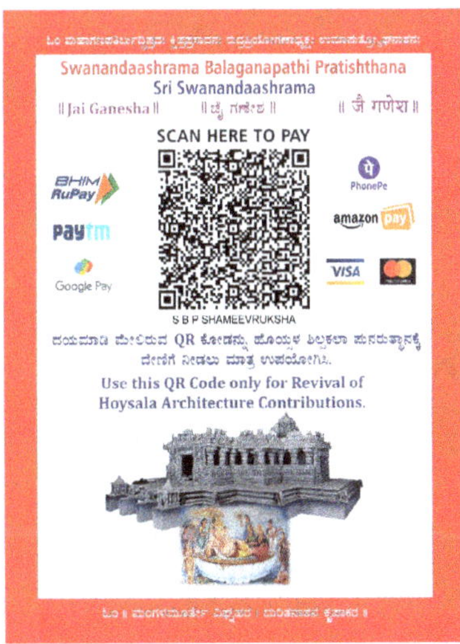

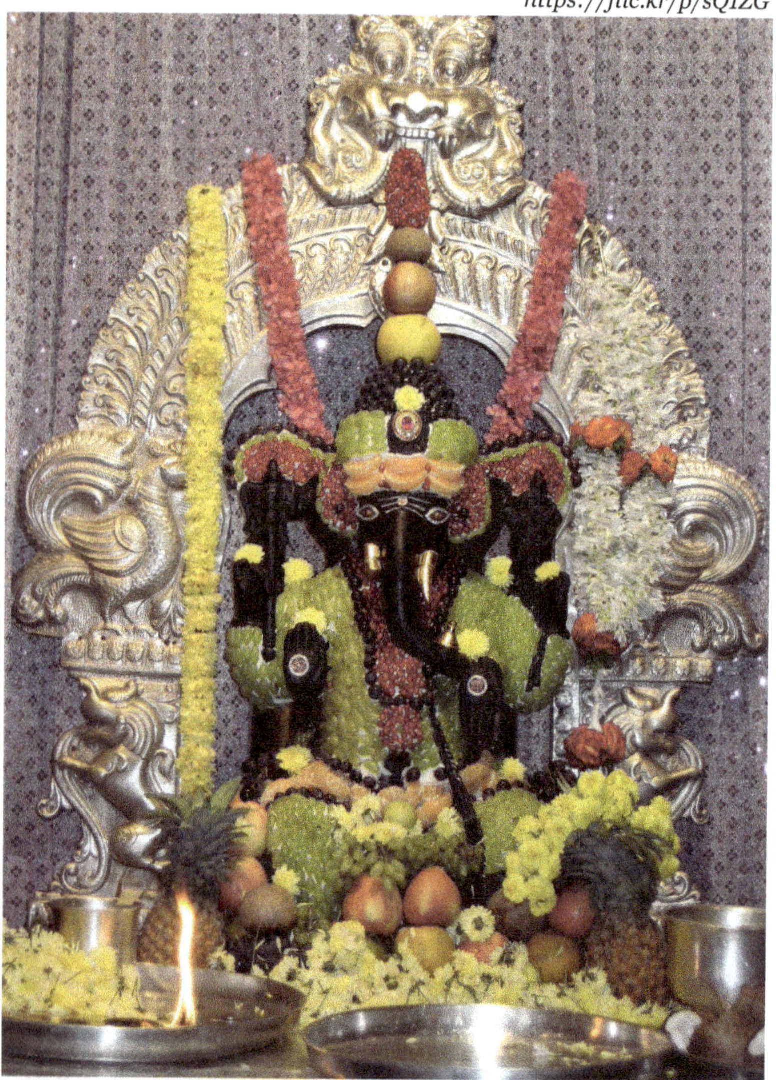

Sri Varasiddhi Vināyaka, Jayanagar 4th Block, Bengaluru

Introduction

ಓಂ ಮಹಾಗಣಪತಿರ್ಬುದ್ಧಿಪ್ರದಃ ಕ್ಷಿಪ್ರಪ್ರಸಾದನಃ |
ರುದ್ರಪ್ರಿಯೋಗಣಾಧ್ಯಕ್ಷಃ ಉಮಾಪುತ್ರೋ ಅಘನಾಶನಃ ||

In the late 1990s, HPR and self met Santhosh Rāvel outside this
wonderful temple late one night. HPR met his match in a
person who could just keep on talking! And the discussion
went on way past midnight

I met Rāvel again in Jayanagar 3rd Block early November 1999
at a function to celebrate Ganesha, where he graciously invited
my family for Diwali at Swānandāshrama that year, saying that
visiting the Bāla Gaṇapati (now called the Moola Gaṇapati)
there was very good for kids

We went over that long weekend, with the Diwali holidays on
8th~9th November. On the last day of the holidays, we found a
photo of Ganesha outside our bathroom window. Quite
mysterious, as our Adarsh Gardens flat was on the fourth floor!

Later that month, we did the ground-breaking for our house in
Whitefield

Ever since then, we have been visiting Swānandāshrama and
enjoying the company of Rāvel and many other devotees

ಓಂ ಮಂಗಳಮೂರ್ತೇ ವಿಘ್ನಹರ |
ದುರಿತನಾಶನ ಕೃಪಾಕರ ||

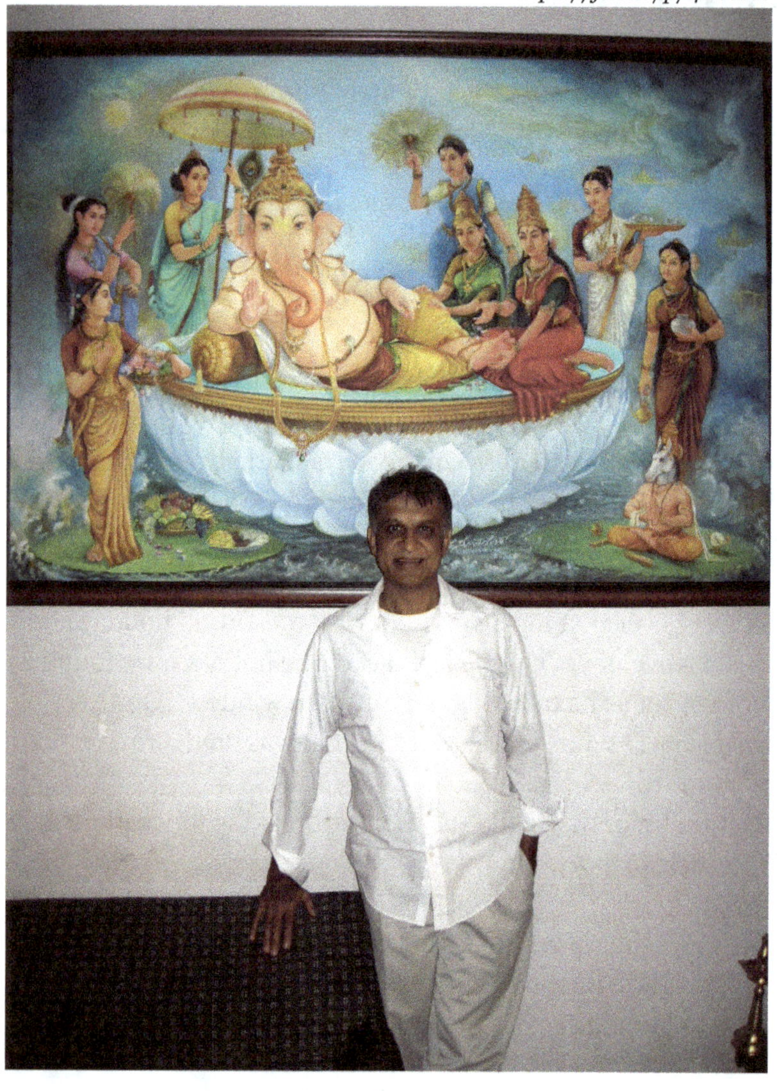

Prime Mover behind Swānandāshrama

Santhosh Rāvel is the prime mover behind Swānandāshrama and the lynch-pin of all its activities, ever since it started on Akshaya Tritiya in 1990 (Friday 27th April)

He meets everyone cheerfully and gives out a lot of love and everyone is touched by it. The main reason for that is his great ability to see Swānanda in everyone

When Swami first came to Bengaluru in 1944, he stayed at the house of Sri R Seshagiri Rao, his grandfather. Rāvel was a member of Swami's bhajan troupe, but he used to sing Ganesha songs at random and upset the other singers! It's safe to say that Swānanda speaks through Rāvel. With little training, he's composed lovely songs, inspired by Swānanda

In 1990, he donated the ten-acre property on which Swānandāshrama is coming to life

Behind this happy-go-lucky attitude, Rāvel is very focused, like Stanley Kubrick:

"I don't know what I want, but I certainly know what I don't want"

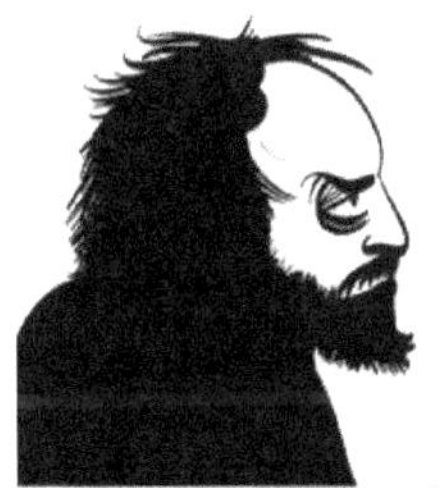

© Antony Hare

When i met Rāvel at Swānandāshrama May 2006, he was mentioning how people were flocking there

In one case, a little girl couldn't speak for a long time and her parents brought her to Swānanda. Later, in a dream, Rāvel saw Swānanda inscribing an ॐ on the tongue of a little girl and soon she started speaking!

Later, Rāvel was narrating how he felt the life-force when he visited Viṭhōbā at ⦿ Pandharpur . He didn't feel it was a statue, he felt that it was a great living being

---

During a visit to his house mid December 2008, Rāvel narrated how he came under the influence of Swānanda [Bāla Gaṇapati]

Once he took a vow that he wouldn't eat anything till Swānanda revealed His form in the **physical** world

For two days, there was no sign and our man Rāvel went w/o food

Come the third day, between 5:45 and 5:50 AM, he had a dream in which he was driving (he doesn't, in our world) with four others of his Swānanda group and saw a Brahminy Kite (locally called **Garuḍa**) following them incessantly

As the others craned their necks to see it (all from the same window!), the speck became bigger and bigger and as it got closer, it morphed into an awesome Ganesha

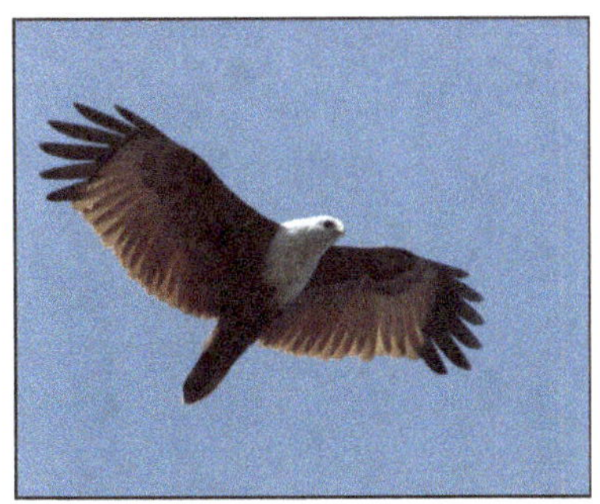

All of them were awestruck as Swānanda, hovering in the air, blessed them with His trunk, **chuckling at the five faces in the same window**

That woke him up and he ran outside in the morning mist to see a Garuḍa circling over his house. His piercing scream "Ganesha" woke up the neighborhood!

Ever since then, for devotees of Swānanda out on a task, the sight of a Garuḍa is a sure sign of success

When i see a Garuḍa at the start of travel, i treat it as an indication of good things to happen

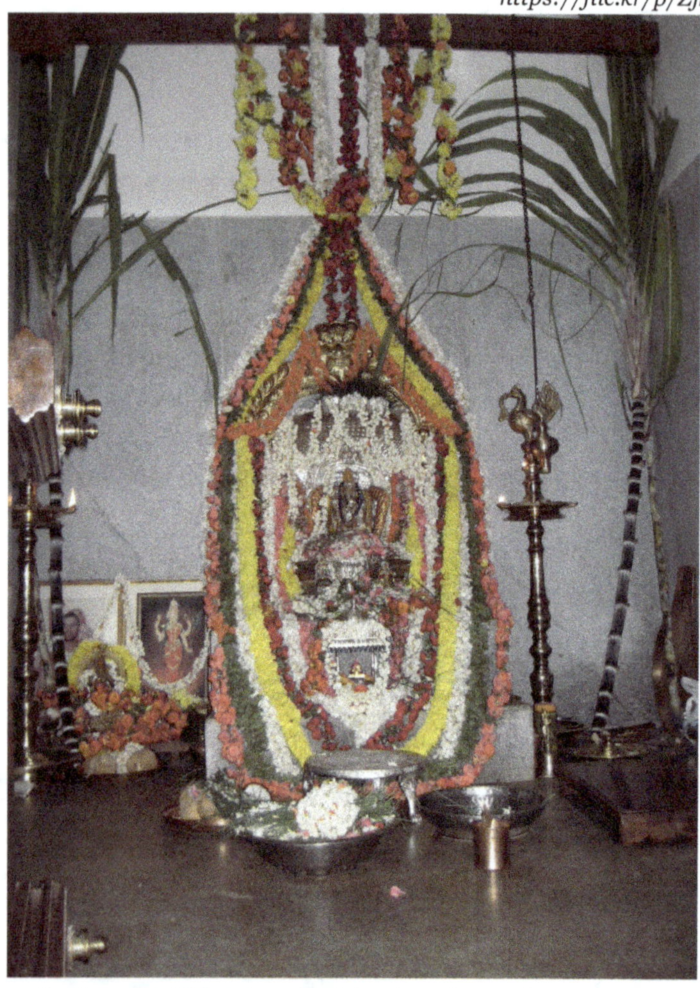

Swānanda Bāla Gaṇapati during the MahāGaṇapati
Panchāyatana Temple Inauguration

Visits to Swānandāshrama

This section covers a few visits to Swānandāshrama in various contexts. They were done in the 2000s and much would have changed by now, but the reader can get a general idea of what to expect

Ranga Pooja

This is my favorite pooja at Swānandāshrama, which is done the night of the Full Moon. All the lamps create a mystical air and the Full Moon adds to the magic

A particularly special one was on the birth centenary of John Steinbeck, my favorite American author, on Wednesday 27th February 2002

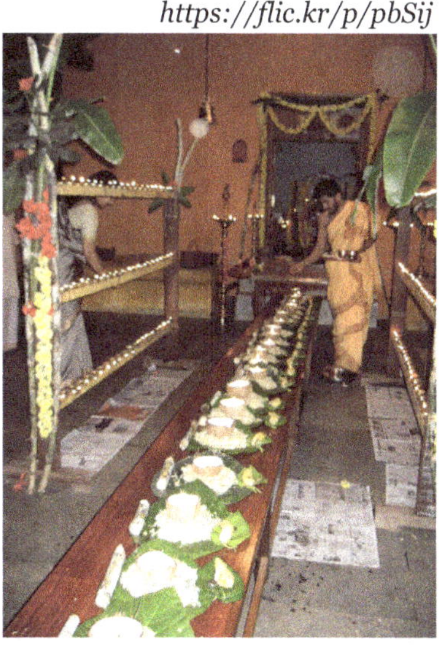
https://flic.kr/p/pbSij

Since the number **21** is dear to Swānanda, there are 21 half-coconuts, with ghee wicks inside them, which we light

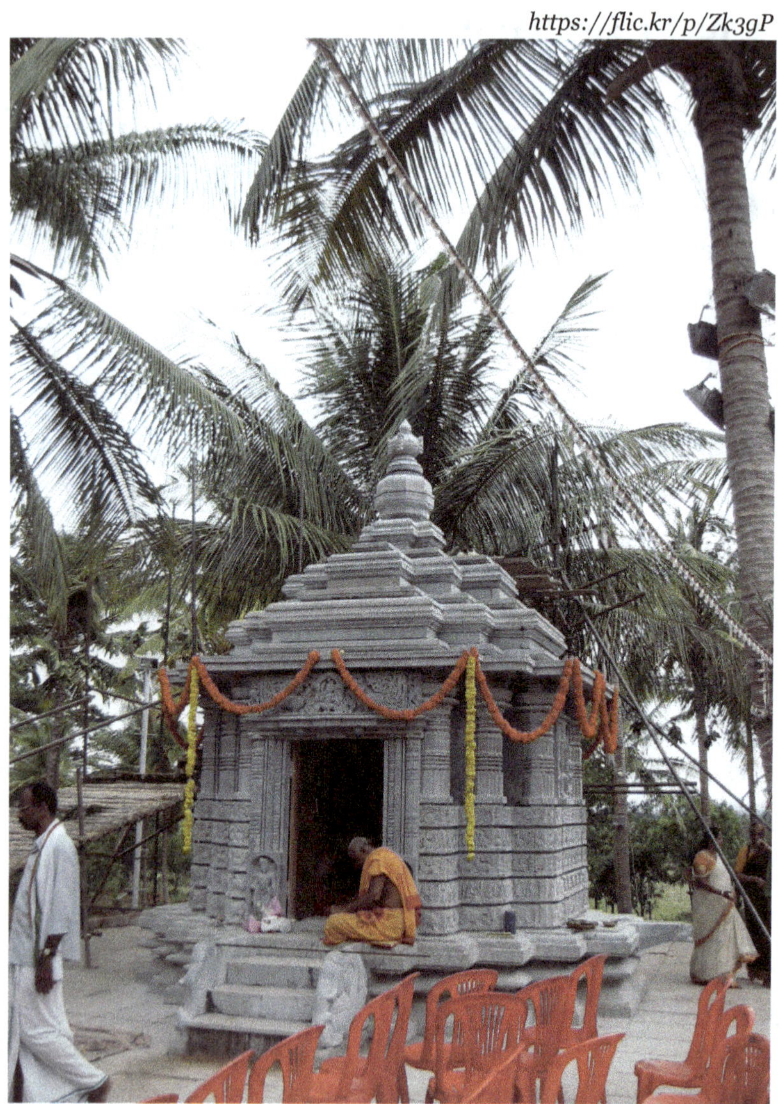

MahāGaṇapati Panchāyatana Temple

Had promised Team Swānanda that we would donate ₹1M as soon as the shares were released by Infosys after the ESOP tax challenge, which was going on from the late 1990s, was resolved. The shares were released early 2007 and we could make our contribution

A MahāGaṇapati temple is the first to be built in any mammoth endeavor, such as the one being undertaken at Swānandāshrama

This was duly built in the *Hoysaḷa* architecture style and was consecrated towards the end of June 2007, which visit we enjoyed thoroughly

It's the first one built in the *Hoysaḷa* style after the Belur~Halebid temple, which construction started around 1121 CE and was completed in 1160 CE

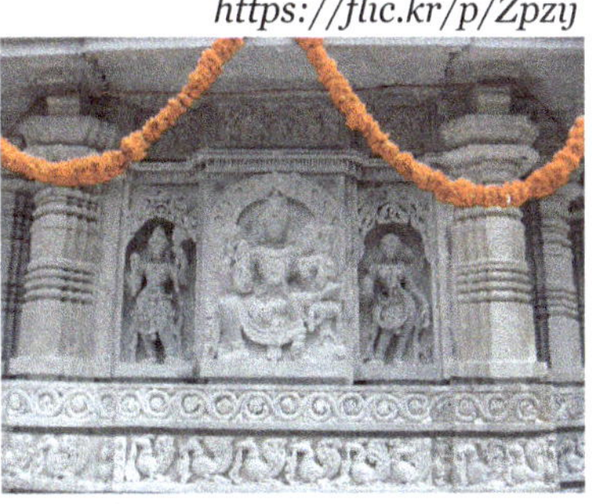

https://flic.kr/p/Zpzij

Detail on Temple

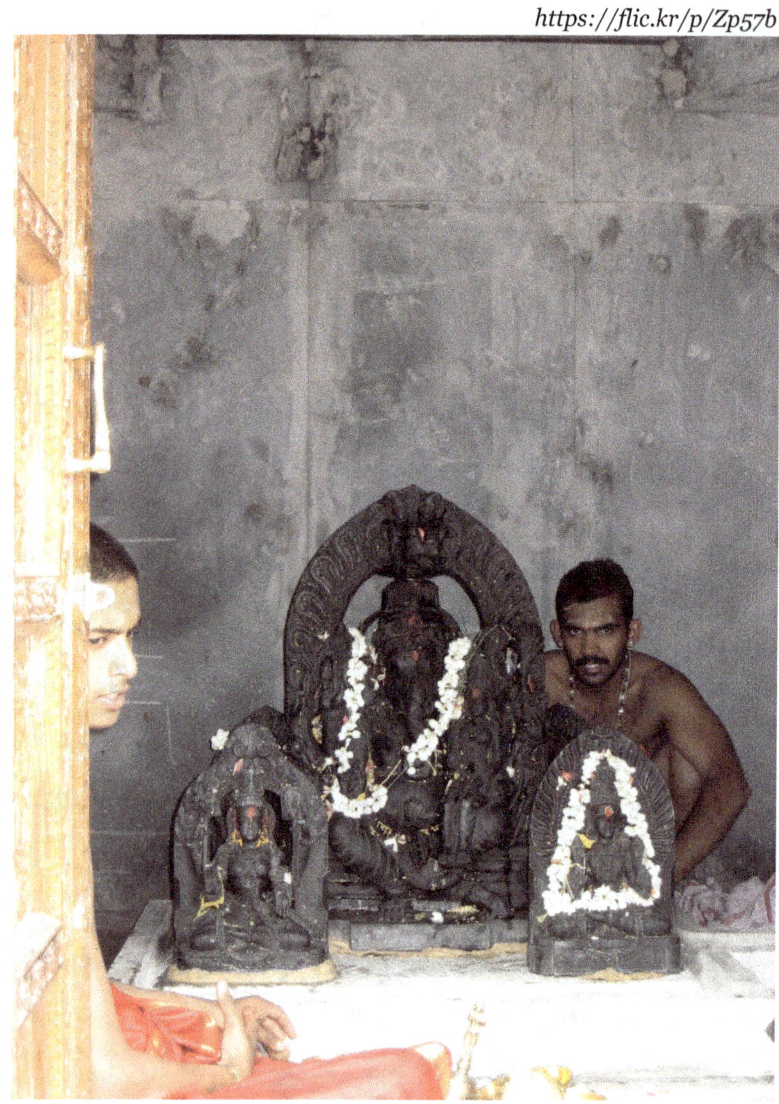

Later, i particularly liked the discourse given by the Swāmiji of Swānandāshrama, where he explained the significance of the five deities in the temple:

- Surya (right), for *ārōgya* [a healthy state]
- MahāGaṇapati (center), for *nirvighna* (smooth, without obstacles)
- Ambika (left), for *aishwarya* [prosperity]
- Shiva (behind Ambika), for *jñāna*, nicely clarifying along the way that, while it was Saraswati for *jñāna* about everyday things (say, mechanical engineering), it was Lord Shiva for knowledge about Brahmn, the Self
- Vishnu (behind Surya), for *moksha* [liberation]

Enjoyed the discourse quite a bit, even though my Kannada is quite rudimentary

Though it was almost 2 PM, the most important part of the function wasn't evident. Everyone i asked had a different answer: "Finish studies by year-end", "Big Temple soon", etc. Only Rāvel cottoned on to my query and said: "Lunch would be served soon". And it was quite a delectable fare, made sweeter by the wait

On the way out, i was mentioning to Rāvel that the crowd had grown quite a bit and Swānanda had lost its cozy little charm (like when Infosys became an enterprise). He agreed, but said that one had to go with the flow, with the Chief Minister of Karnataka dropping in suddenly the earlier evening!

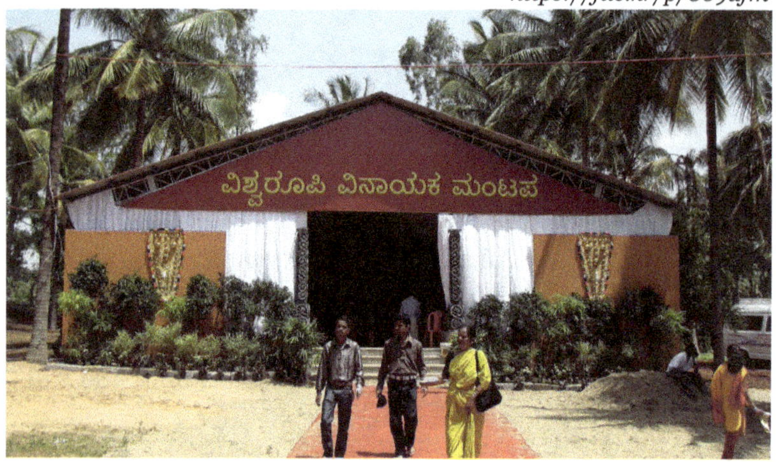

https://flic.kr/p/869ufm

VishwaRoopi Vināyaka Maṇṭapa

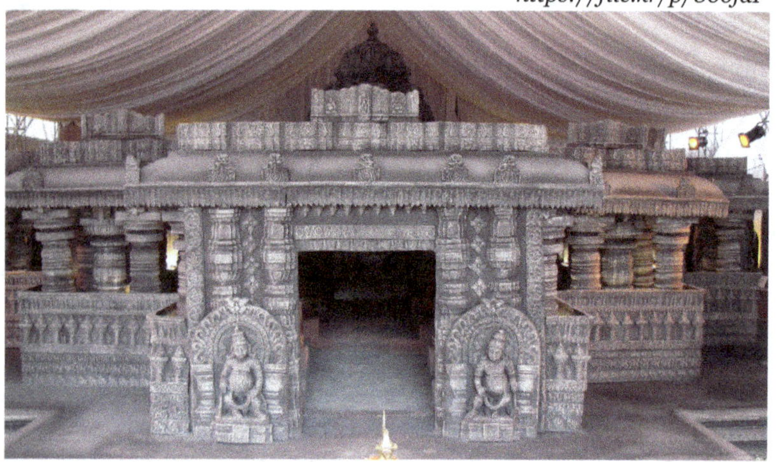

https://flic.kr/p/866jdP

Model of Swānanda Gaṇapati Dēvasthāna

Vishwaroopi Vināyaka Maṇṭapa

Sunday 30th May 2010, we attended the Śilānyāsa function at Swānandāshrama, which showcased the VishwaRoopi Vināyaka Maṇṭapa and how the planned Gaṇapati Dēvasthāna would look (facing page)

As of the compilation of this book, we have:

https://www.swananda.org/

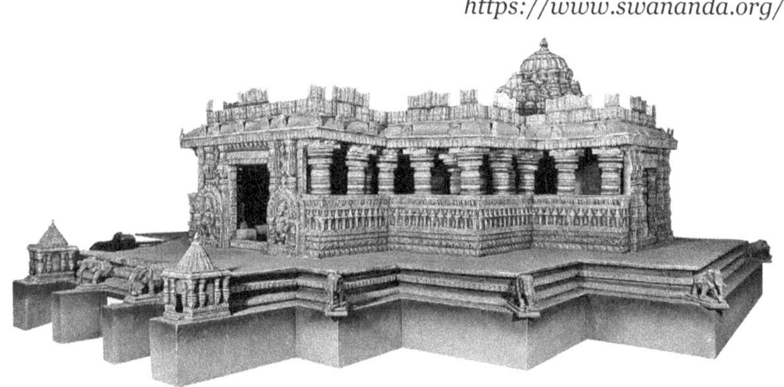

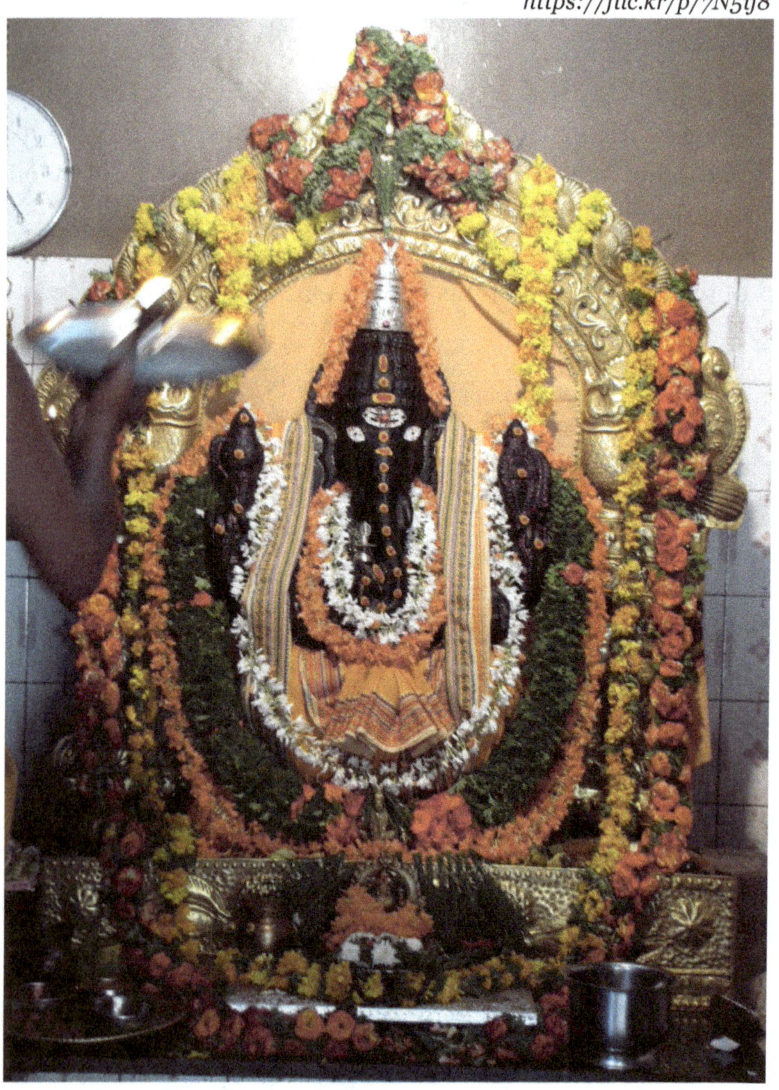

MahaGanapati in Whitefield

A Gaṇapati Mantra

Our knowledge is a little island
in a great ocean of non-knowledge
~Isaac Bashevis Singer

I understood the real power of a mantra through this experience

I got a Gaṇapati mantra from a person called Yerramsetti, whom i met at the Whitefield Gaṇapati temple around the end of March 2004

He said it was a very powerful mantra

Innocently and without too much processing, i started chanting it. Within **two** weeks, we had a solid windfall when Infosys declared its 1:3 bonus and ₹100 dividend per share on Tuesday 13th April 2004, for crossing $1B in revenue

When i told Yerramsetti about it, he said: "Oh, I better start chanting it"!

I still chant it 21 times daily

ॐ *Swānanda*

Here's the mantra in various scripts:

Romanized   संस्कृतम्

Romanized	संस्कृतम्
ōm ēkadantāya vidmahē vakratunḍāya dhīmahi tannō dantiḥ pracōdayāt	ओं एकदंताय विद्महे वक्रतुंडाय धीमहि तन्नो दंतिः प्रचोदयात्
ōm śṭīm krīm klam klam kam gaṇapatayē namaḥ kaṃ gaṇapatayē vara varada guru guru swāhā	ओं श्टीं क्रीं क्लं क्लं कं गणपतये नमः कं गणपतये वर वरद गुरु गुरु स्वाहा
haṃ, sām, dam, nam, yam, ram, ham, śṭīm, śṭīm, śṭīm śṭīm, śṭīm, śṭīm śṭīm, śṭīm, śṭīm gaṇapatayē namaḥ	हं, सां, दं, नं, यं, रं, हं, श्टीं, श्टीं, श्टीं, श्टीं, श्टीं, श्टीं, श्टीं, श्टीं, श्टीं, गणपतये नमः

ಕನ್ನಡ

ಓಂ ಏಕದಂತಾಯ ವಿದ್ಮಹೇ
ವಕ್ರತುಂಡಾಯ ಧೀಮಹಿ
ತನ್ನೋ ದಂತಿಃ ಪ್ರಚೋದಯಾತ್

ಓಂ ಶ್ರೀಂ ಕ್ರೀಂ ಕ್ಲಂ ಕ್ಲಂ ಕಂ ಗಣಪತಯೇ
ನಮಃ
ಕಂ ಗಣಪತಯೇ ವರ ವರದ ಗುರು
ಗುರು ಸ್ವಾಹಾ

ಹಂ, ಸಾಂ, ದಂ, ನಂ, ಯಂ, ರಂ, ಹಂ,
ಶ್ರೀಂ, ಶ್ರೀಂ, ಶ್ರೀಂ,
ಶ್ರೀಂ, ಶ್ರೀಂ, ಶ್ರೀಂ,
ಶ್ರೀಂ, ಶ್ರೀಂ, ಶ್ರೀಂ,
ಗಣಪತಯೇ ನಮಃ

తెలుగు

ఓం ఏకదంతాయ విద్మహే
వక్రతుండాయ ధీమహి
తన్నో దంతిః ప్రచోదయాత్

ఓం శ్రీం క్రీం క్లం క్లం కం గణపతయె
నమః
కం గణపతయె వర వరద గురు గురు
స్వాహ్

హాం, సాం, దం, నం, యం, రం, హాం,
శ్రీం, శ్రీం, శ్రీం,
శ్రీం, శ్రీం, శ్రీం,
శ్రీం, శ్రీం, శ్రీం,
గణపతయె నమః

മലയാളം

ഓം ഏകദന്താായ വിദ്മഹേ
വക്രതുണ്ഡായ ധീമഹി
തന്നോ ദന്തിഃ പ്രചോദയാത്

ഓം ശാരീം ക്രീം ക്ലാം ക്ലം കാം
ഗണപതയേ നമഃ
കം ഗണപതയേ വര വരദ
ഗുരു ഗുരു സ്വാഹാ

ഹാം, സാം, ഡാം, നാം, യാം,
റാം, ഹാം,
ക്ലീം, ക്ലീം, ക്ലീം
ക്ലീം, ക്ലീം, ക്ലീം
ക്ലീം, ക്ലീം, ക്ലീം
ക്ലീം, ക്ലീം, ക്ലീം
ഗണപതയേ നമഃ

தமிழ்

ஓம் ஏகத₃ந்தாய வித்₃மஹே
வக்ரத்துண்டா₃ய தீ₄மஹி
தந்நோ த₃ந்தி:
ப்ரசோத₃யாத்

ஓம் ஶ்ரீம், க்ரீம் க்லம் க்லம்
கம் க₃ணபதயே நம:
கம் க₃ணபதயே வர வரத₃
க்₃ரு க்₃ரு
ஸ்வாஹ்ரா/ஸ்வாஹ்ர

ஹம், ஸாம், த₃ம், நம், யம்,
ரம், ஹம்
ஶ்ரீம், ஶ்ரீம், ஶ்ரீம்,
ஶ்ரீம், ஶ்ரீம், ஶ்ரீம்
க₃ணபதயே நம:

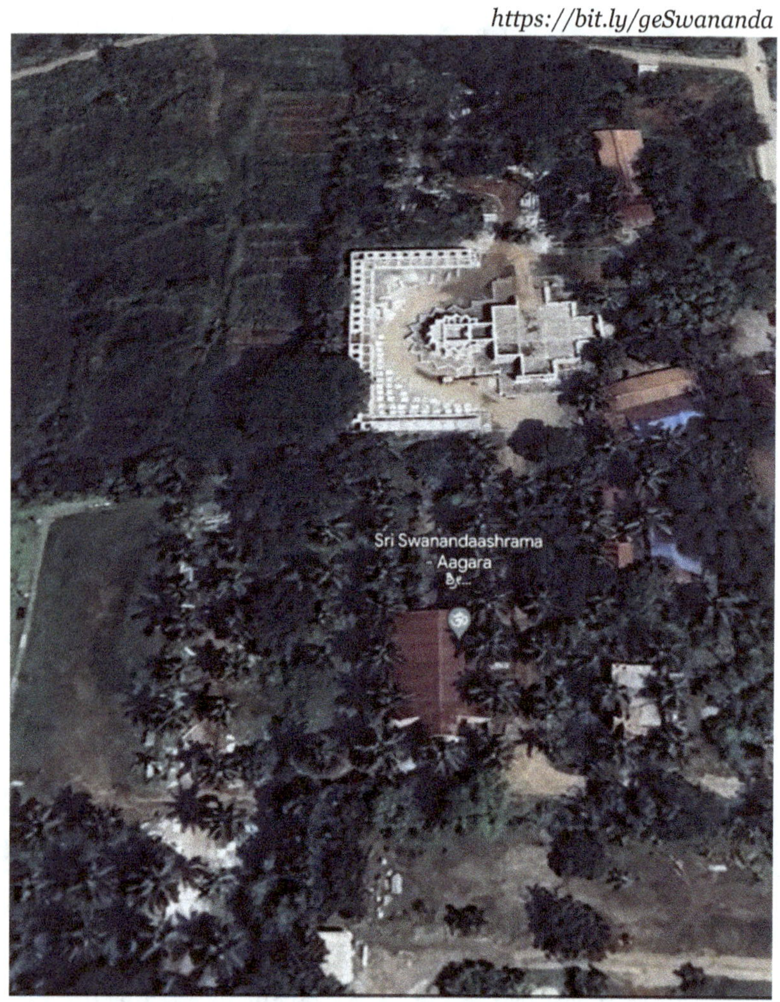

Sri Swānandāshrama in Google Earth

Gaṇapati Dēvasthāna

The Swānanda Gaṇapati Dēvasthāna [abode of the Gods] will house:

- 32 Gaṇapati of various forms, each weighing ~350 kg
- Four Gaṇapati pertaining to the four *yuga* (*krita*, *tretā*, *dvāpara*, and *kali*); each weighing ~500 kg

Salient features of this temple complex:

- *Hoysaḷa* style of Architecture, a testimony to our glorious culture
- Recreated authentically, **after 750 years**
- Being conceptualized and crafted by a rich group of committed experts
- 16/32 pointed star-shaped ground plan
- Visual treat / spiritual experience that pulls one repeatedly back to the temple
- Highly decorative and exuberant style
- Narrative sculptures

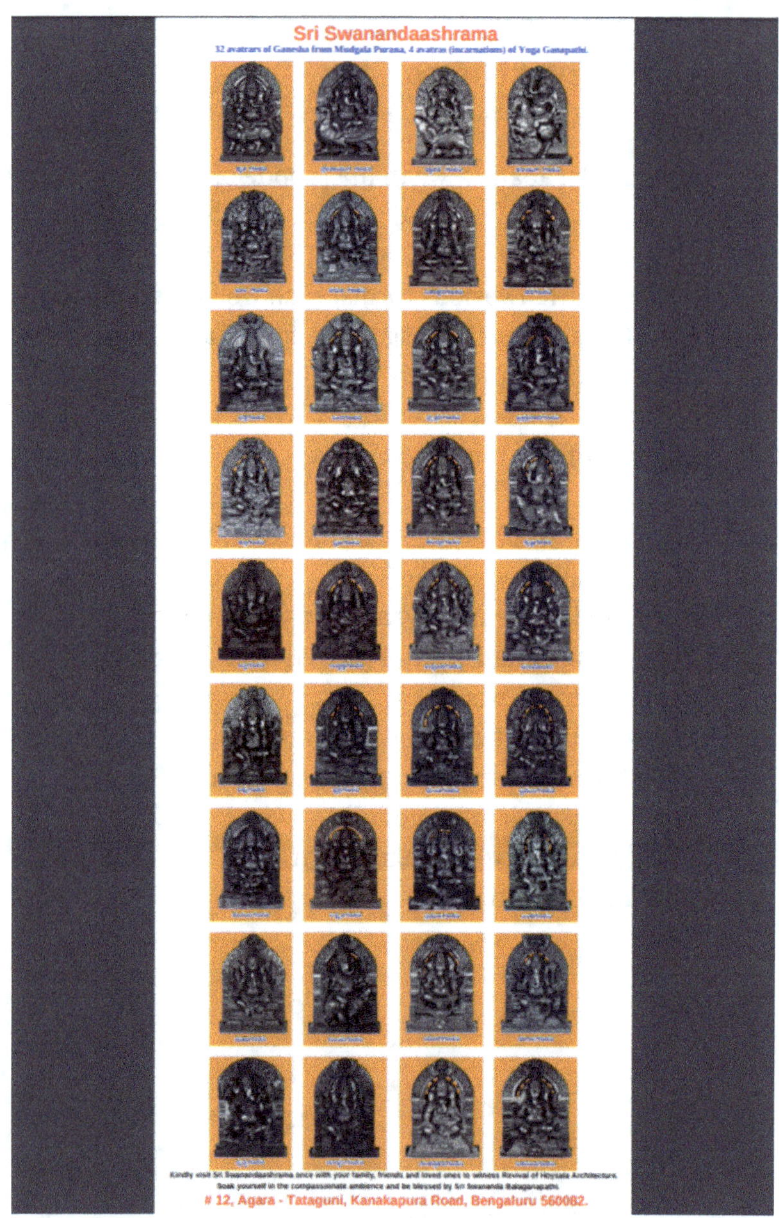

Sri Swanandaashrama
32 avatars of Ganesha from Mudgala Purana, 4 avatras (incarnations) of Yuga Ganapathi.
Kindly visit Sri Swanandaashrama once with your family, friends and loved ones to witness Revival of Hoysala Architecture. Soak yourself in the compassionate ambience and be blessed by Sri Swananda Balaganapathi.
12, Agara - Tataguni, Kanakapura Road, Bengaluru 560082.

For each of the 32 Gaṇapati, the following will be provided:

- An image of the Gaṇapati at Swānandāshrama
- The *dhyāna śloka*, which describes the deity and helps devotees to bring the deity in their mind and proceed with meditation, for the Gaṇapati in Kannada script
  - Its meaning in English
  - *upāsana phala* [beneficial effects of chanting it]

This set will be followed by the Gaṇapati for the four *yuga* [epoch]:

https://g.co/kgs/AHsxDs

- *Satya yuga* aka *Krita yuga*
- *Tretāyuga*
- *Dvāpara yuga*
- *Kali yuga*, the one running currently

Here's the Gaṇapati suggested for you based on the *nakshatra* [star] at the time of your birth:

Nakshatra	Suggested Gaṇapati
Aśvinī - अश्विनी	06. ಶ್ರೀ ದ್ವಿಜ ಗಣಪತಿ (Śrī Dvija Gaṇapati)
Bharaṇī - भरणी	07. ಶ್ರೀ ಸಿದ್ಧಿ ಗಣಪತಿ (Śrī Siddhi Gaṇapati)
Krittika - कृत्तिका	08. ಶ್ರೀ ಉಚ್ಛಿಷ್ಟ ಗಣಪತಿ (Śrī Ucçhishṭa Gaṇapati)
Rōhiṇī - रोहिणी	09. ಶ್ರೀ ವಿಘ್ನ ಗಣಪತಿ (Śrī Vighna Gaṇapati)
Mrigaśirā - मृगशिर	10. ಶ್ರೀ ಕ್ಷಿಪ್ರ ಗಣಪತಿ (Śrī Kshipra Gaṇapati)
Ardra - आर्द्रा	11. ಶ್ರೀ ಹೇರಂಬ ಗಣಪತಿ (Śrī Heramba Gaṇapati)
Punarvasu - पुनर्वसु	12. ಶ್ರೀ ಲಕ್ಷ್ಮೀ ಗಣಪತಿ (Śrī Lakṣmī Gaṇapati)
Pushya - पुष्य	13. ಶ್ರೀ ಮಹಾ ಗಣಪತಿ (Śrī Mahā Gaṇapati)
Āśleṣā - आश्ळेषा/आश्लेषा	14. ಶ್ರೀ ವಿಜಯ ಗಣಪತಿ (Śrī Vijaya Gaṇapati)
Maghā - मघा	15. ಶ್ರೀ ನೃತ್ಯ ಗಣಪತಿ (Śrī Nṛtya Gaṇapati)

Nakshatra	**Suggested Gaṇapati**
Pūrva Phālguṇī - पूर्व फाल्गुनी	16. ಶ್ರೀ ಉೂರ್ಧ್ವ ಗಣಪತಿ (Śrī Ūrdhva Gaṇapati)
Uttara Phālguṇī - उत्तर फाल्गुनी	17. ಶ್ರೀ ಏಕಾಕ್ಷರ ಗಣಪತಿ (Śrī Ekākshara Gaṇapati)
Hasta - हस्त	18. ಶ್ರೀ ವರ ಗಣಪತಿ (Śrī Vara Gaṇapati)
Chitrā - चित्रा	19. ಶ್ರೀ ತ್ರ್ಯಕ್ಷರ ಗಣಪತಿ (Śrī Tryakshara Gaṇapati)
Svāti - स्वाति	20. ಶ್ರೀ ಕ್ಷಿಪ್ರಪ್ರಸಾದ ಗಣಪತಿ (Śrī KshipraPrasāda Gaṇapati)
Viśākhā - विशाखा	21. ಶ್ರೀ ಹರಿದ್ರಾ ಗಣಪತಿ (Śrī Haridrā Gaṇapati)
Anurādha - अनुराधा	22. ಶ್ರೀ ಏಕದಂತ ಗಣಪತಿ (Śrī Ekadanta Gaṇapati)
Jyeṣṭā - ज्येष्ठा	23. ಶ್ರೀ ಸೃಷ್ಟಿ ಗಣಪತಿ (Śrī Sṛishṭi Gaṇapati)
Mūla - मूल	24. ಶ್ರೀ ಉದ್ದಂಡ ಗಣಪತಿ (Śrī Uddaṇḍa Gaṇapati)
Pūrva Āṣāḍā - पूर्व आषाढ	25. ಶ್ರೀ ಋಣಮೋಚನ ಗಣಪತಿ (Śrī Ṛiṇamochana Gaṇapati)
Uttara Āṣāḍā - उत्तर आषाढ	26. ಶ್ರೀ ಧುಂಡಿ ಗಣಪತಿ (Śrī Dhuṇḍi Gaṇapati)

Nakshatra	**Suggested Gaṇapati**
Śravaṇa - श्रवण	27. ಶ್ರೀ ದ್ವಿಮುಖ ಗಣಪತಿ (Śrī Dvimukha Gaṇapati)
Dhaniṣṭā - धनिष्ठा	28. ಶ್ರೀ ತ್ರಿಮುಖ ಗಣಪತಿ (Śrī Trimukha Gaṇapati)
Śatabhiṣa - शतभिष	29. ಶ್ರೀ ಸಿಂಹ ಗಣಪತಿ (Śrī Simha Gaṇapati)
Pūrva Bhādrapadā - पूर्व भाद्रपदा	30. ಶ್ರೀ ಯೋಗ ಗಣಪತಿ (Śrī Yōga Gaṇapati)
Uttara Bhādrapadā - उत्तर भाद्रपदा	31. ಶ್ರೀ ದುರ್ಗಾ ಗಣಪತಿ (Śrī Durgā Gaṇapati)
Revatī - रेवती	32. ಶ್ರೀ ಸಂಕಟಹರ ಗಣಪತಿ (Śrī Saṇkaṭahara Gaṇapati)

References:

Web Page	**QR Code**

Wikipedia:
Thirty-two forms of Ganesha

Wikipedia:
గణేశుని ముప్పై రెండు రూపాలు

Wikipedia:
List of *nakshatra*

StotraNidhi:
Śloka in various languages
[తెలుగు, ಕನ್ನಡ, தமிழ், देवनागरी,
English (IAST)]

Dvatrimsat Ganapathi
Dhyana Slokah - द्वात्रिंशद्गणपति
ध्यान श्लोकाः

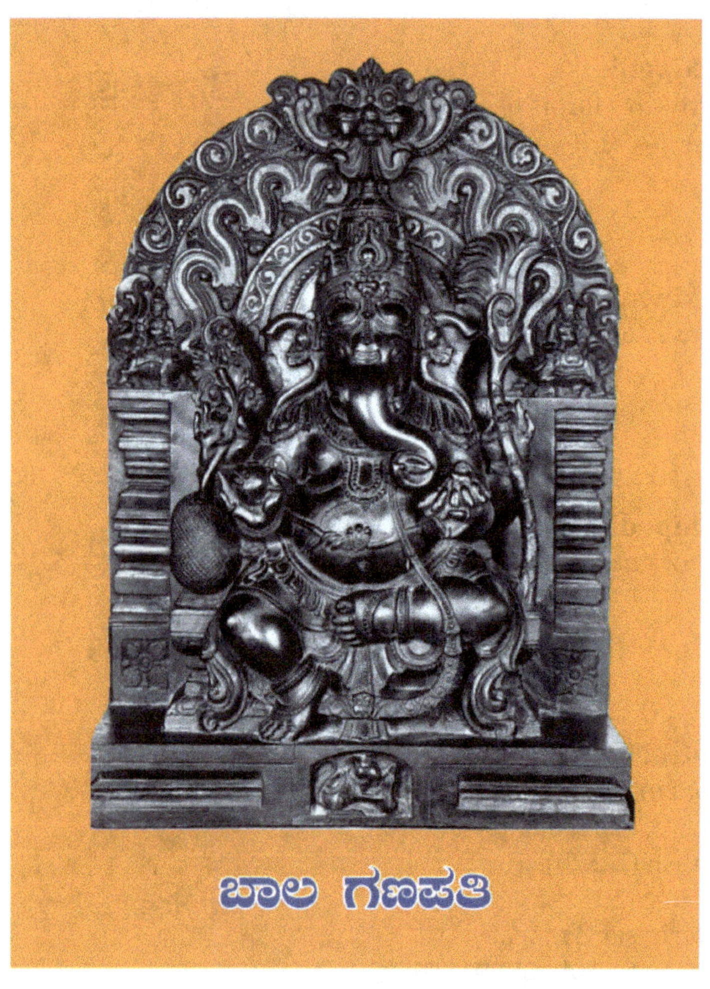

Representing the **Earth Element** (*pañcabhūta prithvi*)

01. ಶ್ರೀ ಬಾಲ ಗಣಪತಿ (Śrī Bāla Gaṇapati)

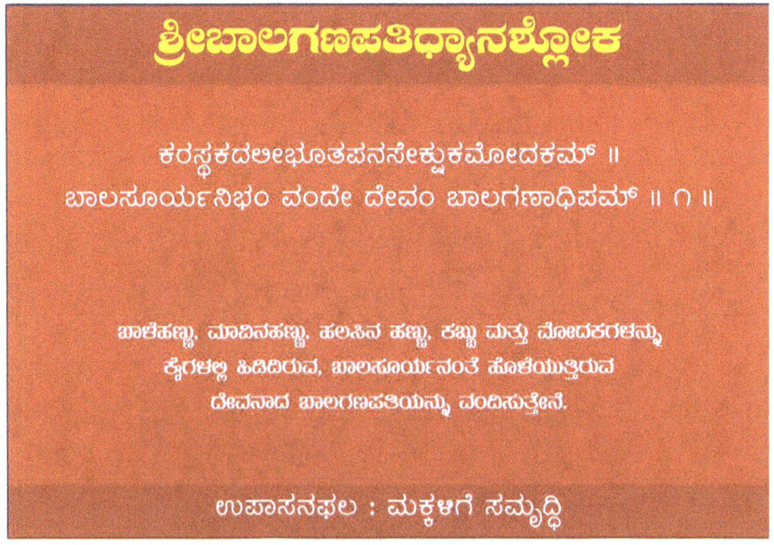

Śrī Bāla Gaṇapati dhyāna śloka

I salute Lord *Bāla Gaṇapati* adorned with a garland of tender flowers, having plantain, mango, jackfruit, sugarcane, and sweets in His hands, and who is effulgent like the rising sun

upāsana phala:
Prosperity of children

Please scan this QR Code to listen to the *dhyāna śloka* in various languages of 🇮🇳

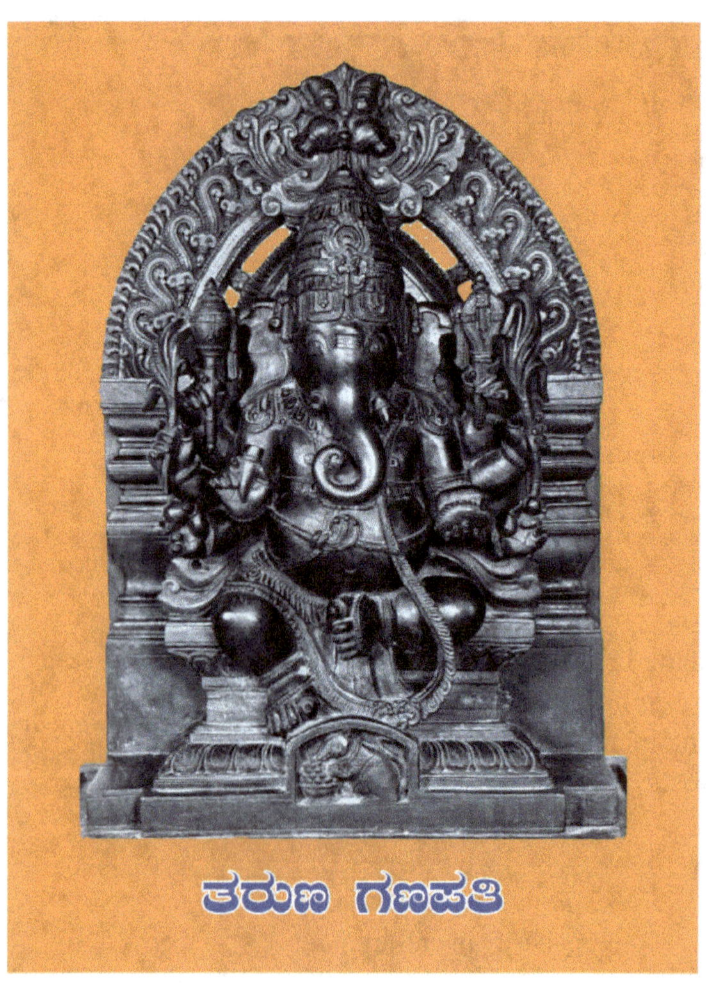

Representing the **Air Element** (*pañcabhūta vāyu*)

02. ಶ್ರೀ ತರುಣ ಗಣಪತಿ (Śrī Taruṇa Gaṇapati)

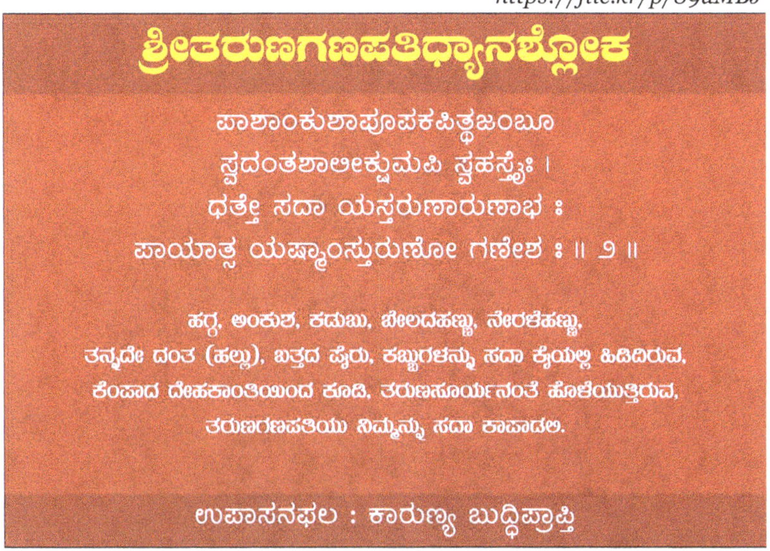

Śrī Taruṇa Gaṇapati dhyāna śloka

May the young Lord *Gaṇapati*, who is carrying in His hands the noose, hook, rice-cake, guava fruit, rose apple, own tusk, bunch of corn ears, and sugarcane and who vividly shines forth with His brilliant Youthfulness, bless you all

upāsana phala:
Compassionate intellect

Please scan this QR Code to listen to the *dhyāna śloka* in various languages of 🇮🇳

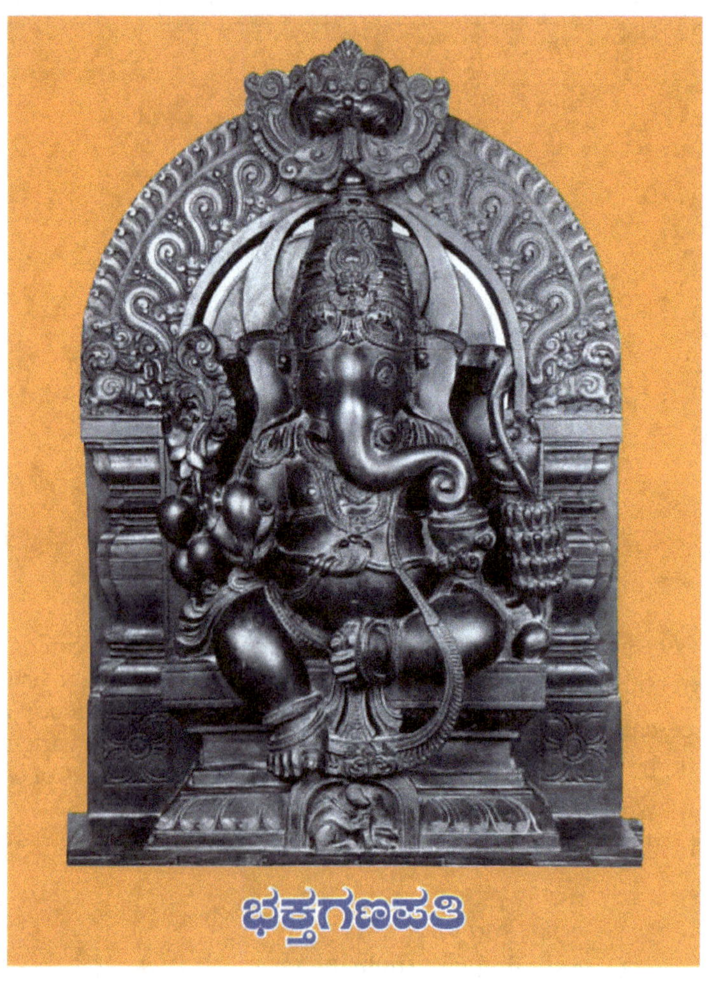

Representing the **Water Element** (*pañcabhūta jala*)

03. ಶ್ರೀ ಭಕ್ತ ಗಣಪತಿ (Śrī Bhakta Gaṇapati)

https://flic.kr/p/89rx74

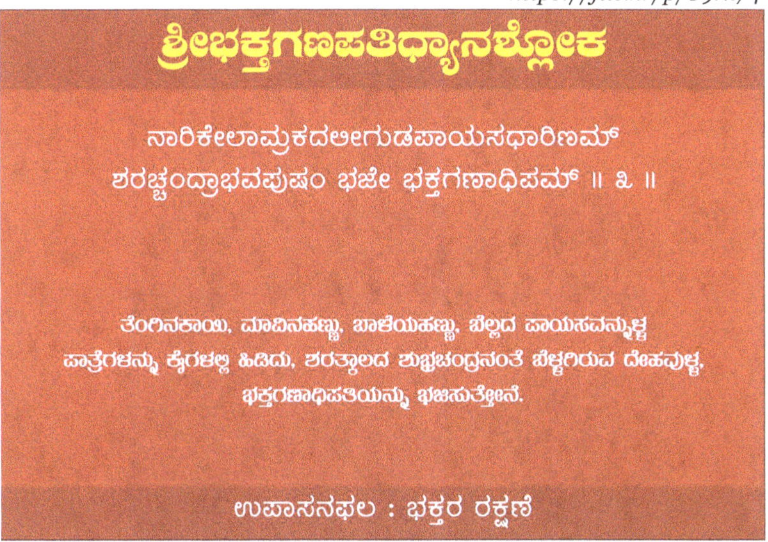

Śrī Bhakta Gaṇapati dhyāna śloka

I worship *Bhakta Gaṇapati*, who is the Lord of His devotees and who shines like the autumn moon, with coconut, mango, plantain, jaggery, and sweets in his hands

upāsana phala:
Protection of Devotees

Please scan this QR Code to listen to the *dhyāna śloka* in various languages of 🇮🇳

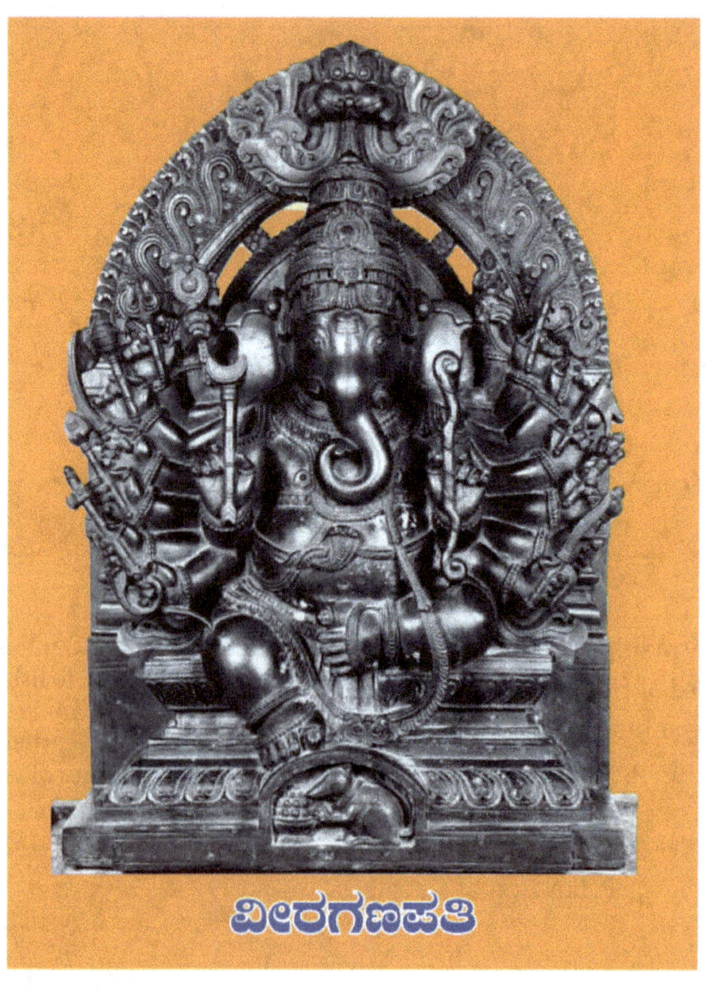

Representing the **Fire Element** (*pañcabhūta agni*)

04. ಶ್ರೀ ವೀರ ಗಣಪತಿ (Śrī Veera Gaṇapati)

https://flic.kr/p/89rx9g

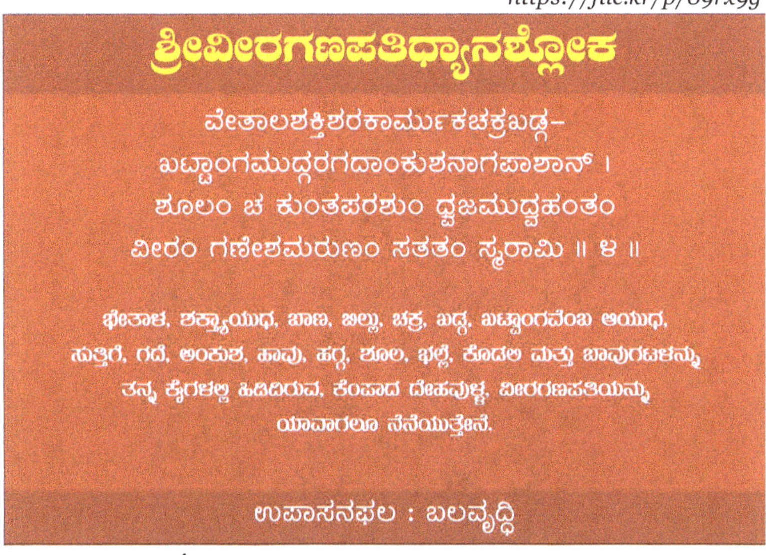

Śrī Veera Gaṇapati dhyāna śloka

I always meditate on the *Veera* (valiant) *Gaṇapati*, who is armed with *Bhātaḷa*, the weapon of power, arrow, bow, wheel, sword, club, hammer, mace, hook, nāgapāśa (serpent noose), spear, plough, and the shining ax

upāsana phala:
Increased strength

Please scan this QR Code to listen to the *dhyāna śloka* in various languages of 🇮🇳

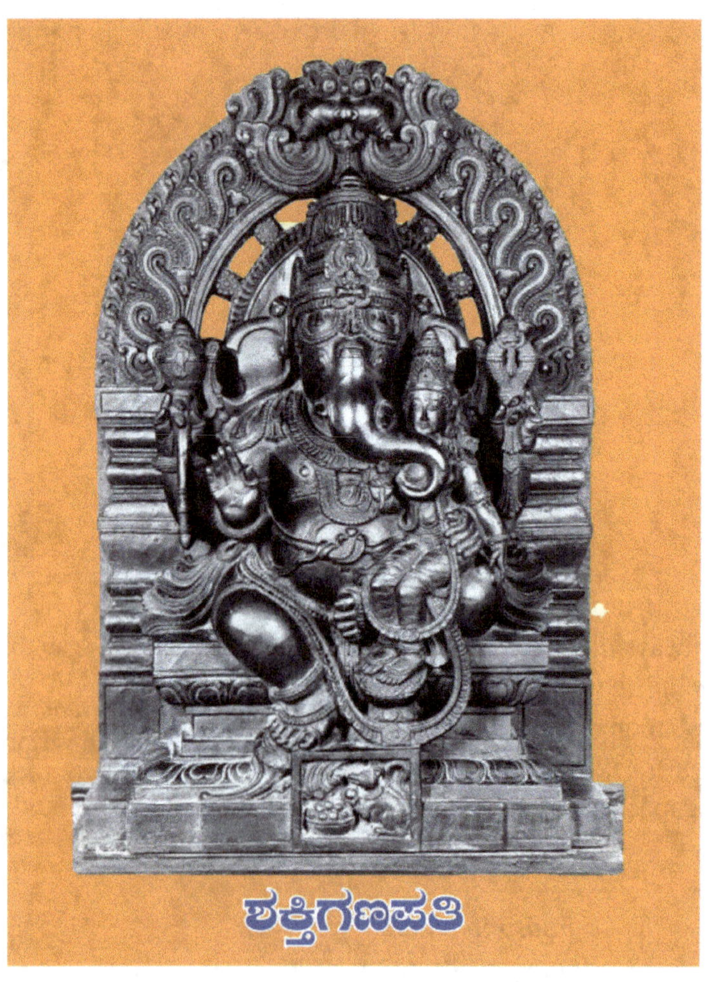

Representing the **Space Element** (*pañcabhūta ākāśa*)

05. ಶ್ರೀ ಶಕ್ತಿ ಗಣಪತಿ (*Śrī Śakti Gaṇapati*)

ಶ್ರೀಶಕ್ತಿಗಣಪತಿಧ್ಯಾನಶ್ಲೋಕ

ಆಲಿಂಗ್ಯ ದೇವೀಂ ಹರಿತಾಂಗಯಷ್ಟಿಂ ಪರಸ್ಪರಾಶ್ಲಿಷ್ಟಕಟಿಪ್ರದೇಶಮ್ ।
ಸಂಧ್ಯಾರುಣಂ ಪಾಶಸೃಣೀ ವಹಂತಂ
ಭಯಾಪಹಂ ಶಕ್ತಿಗಣೇಶಮೀಡೇ ॥ ೫ ॥

ಶಕ್ತಿಯೊಡನಿರುವ ಗಣಪತಿ ಶಕ್ತಿಗಣಪತಿ. ಗಣಪತಿಯು ಹಸುರುಬಣ್ಣವುಳ್ಳ
ತೆಳುದೇಹದ ಶಕ್ತಿದೇವಿಯನ್ನು ಆಲಂಗಿಸಿಕೊಂಡು ಅವಳ ಸೊಂಟವನ್ನು ಬಳಸಿ ಹಿಡಿದಿದ್ದಾನೆ.
ಶಕ್ತಿದೇವಿಯೂ ಸಹ ಗಣಪತಿಯ ಸೊಂಟವನ್ನು ಬಳಸಿ ಹಿಡಿದು ಕೊಂಡಿರುವಳು.
ಸಂಜೆಯ ಕಾಲದ ಕೆಂಬಣ್ಣದಂತೆ ಗಣಪತಿಯ ದೇಹವು ಕೆಂಪಗಿದೆ.
ಹಗ್ಗ ಮತ್ತು ಅಂಕುಶಗಳನ್ನು ಕೈಗಳಲ್ಲಿ ಹಿಡಿದಿದ್ದಾನೆ. (ಭಕ್ತರ) ಭಯಗಳನ್ನು
ದೂರ ಮಾಡುವ ಈ ಶಕ್ತಿಗಣಪತಿಯನ್ನು ನಾನು ಸ್ತೋತ್ರ ಮಾಡುತ್ತೇನೆ.

ಉಪಾಸನಫಲ : ಕಾರ್ಯಸಾಧನೆ

Śrī Śakti Gaṇapati dhyāna śloka

I meditate on Lord *Śakti Gaṇapati*, the destroyer of fear, who is embracing tightly the green complexioned Devi and Whose complexion resembles that of the setting sun and Who is holding noose and rod in His hands

upāsana phala:
Accomplishment of tasks

Please scan this QR Code to listen to the *dhyāna śloka* in various languages of 🇮🇳

ॐ *Swānanda*

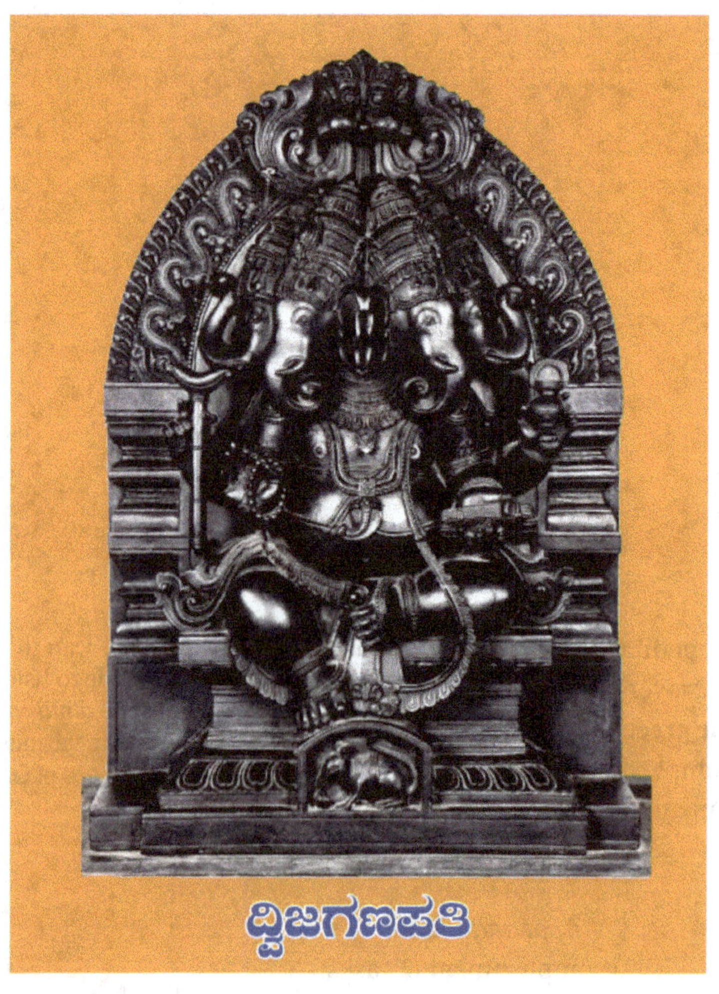

Suggested for those with the birth *nakshatra*
Aśvinī (अश्विनी)

06. ಶ್ರೀ ದ್ವಿಜ ಗಣಪತಿ (Śrī Dvija Gaṇapati)

https://flic.kr/p/89rxeZ

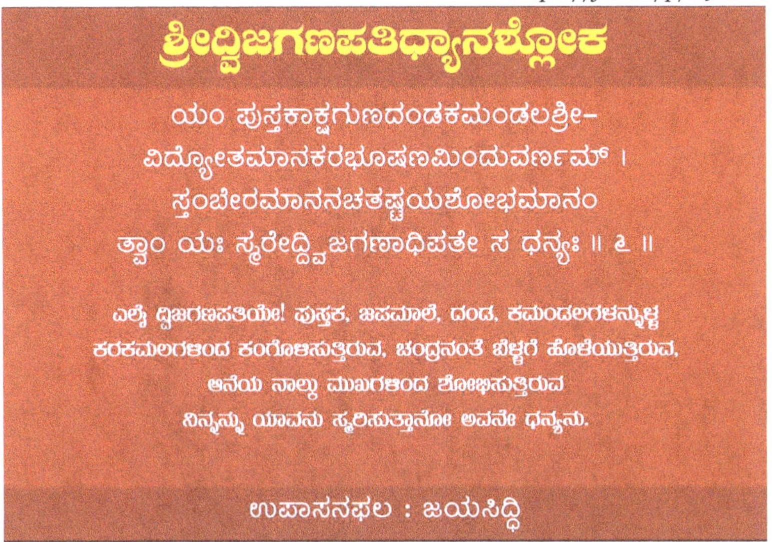

Śrī Dvija Gaṇapati dhyāna śloka

Blessed is he who remembers Thee, O *Dvija Gaṇapati*! Having the book, rosary staff, and *kamaṇḍalu* (water bowl) in Thy hands and endowed with the color of the moon and with the dignity of elephant face

upāsana phala:
Assured Victory

Please scan this QR Code to listen to the *dhyāna śloka* in various languages of 🇮🇳

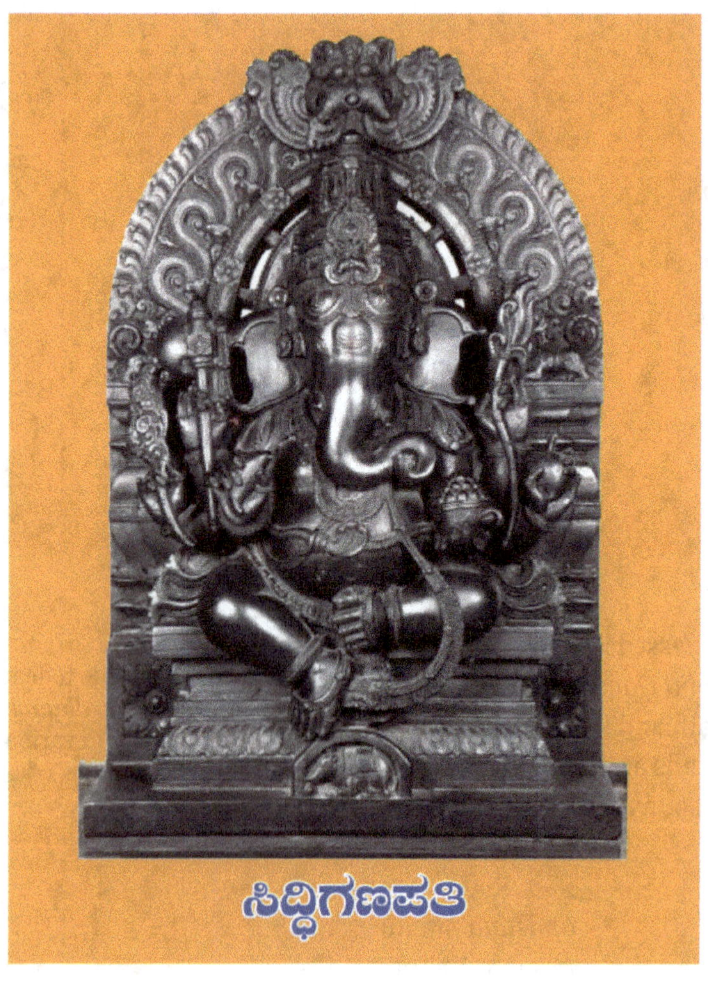

Suggested for those with the birth *nakshatra*
Bharaṇī (भरणी)

07. ಶ್ರೀ ಸಿದ್ಧಿ ಗಣಪತಿ (Śrī Siddhi Gaṇapati)

https://flic.kr/p/89uMPw

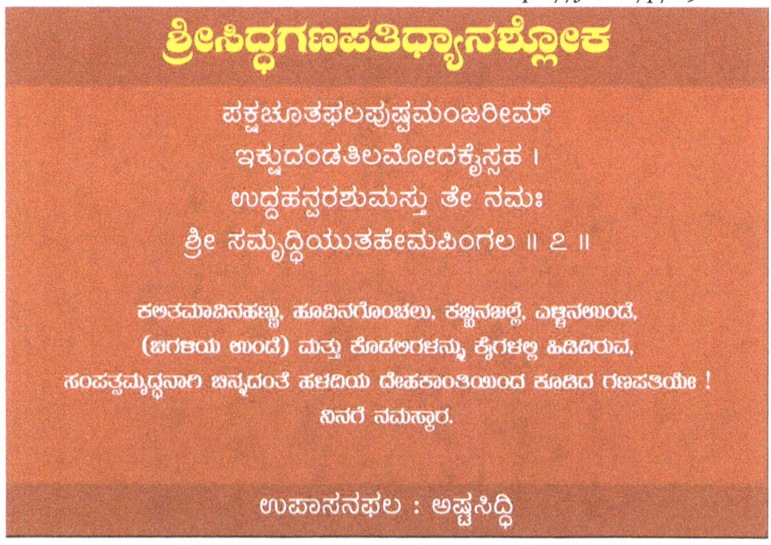

Śrī Siddhi Gaṇapati dhyāna śloka

Salutations to Thee, O golden complexioned *Siddhi Gaṇapati*! Thou endowed with wealth and prosperity and adorning a ripe mango, bunch of flowers, sugarcane, sesame seeds, sweets, and ax in Thy hands

upāsana phala:
Eight Supernatural Powers

Please scan this QR Code to listen to the *dhyāna śloka* in various languages of 🇮🇳

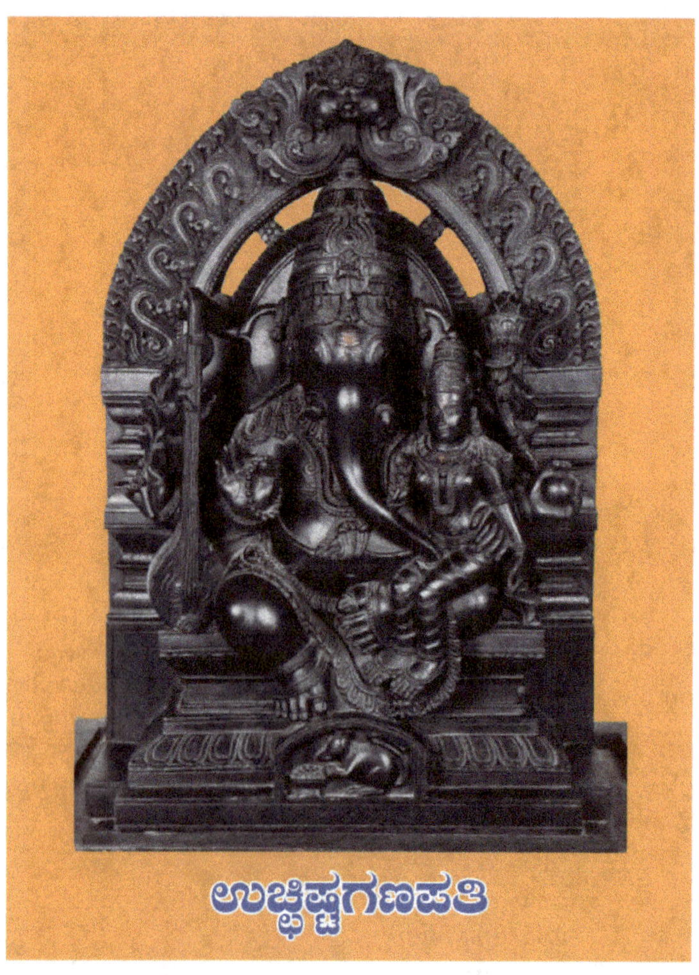

Suggested for those with the birth *nakshatra*
Krittika (कृत्तिका)

08. ಶ್ರೀ ಉಚ್ಛಿಷ್ಟ ಗಣಪತಿ (Śrī Ucçhishṭa Gaṇapati)

https://flic.kr/p/89uMS9

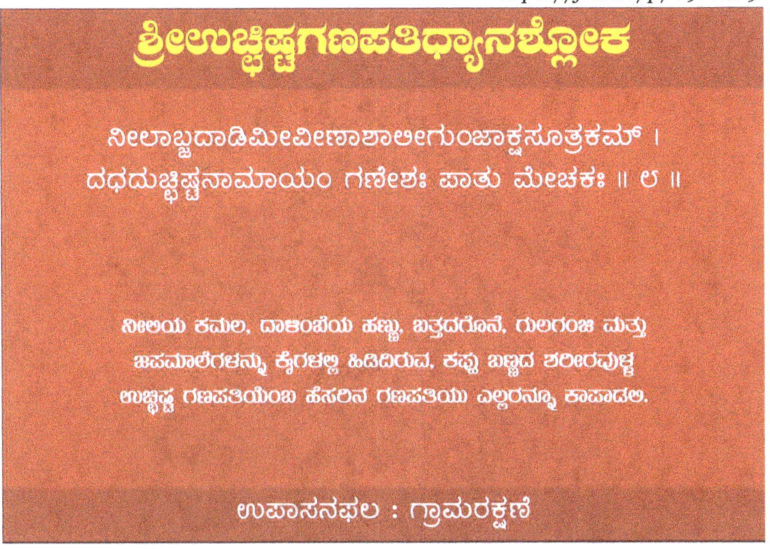

Śrī Ucçhishṭa Gaṇapati dhyāna śloka

May the dark complexioned *Ucçhishṭa Gaṇapati*, having a dark blue lotus, pomegranate fruit, *veena*, corn ears, rosary in His hands, protect me

upāsana phala:
Protection of the precincts

Please scan this QR Code to listen to the *dhyāna śloka* in various languages of 🇮🇳

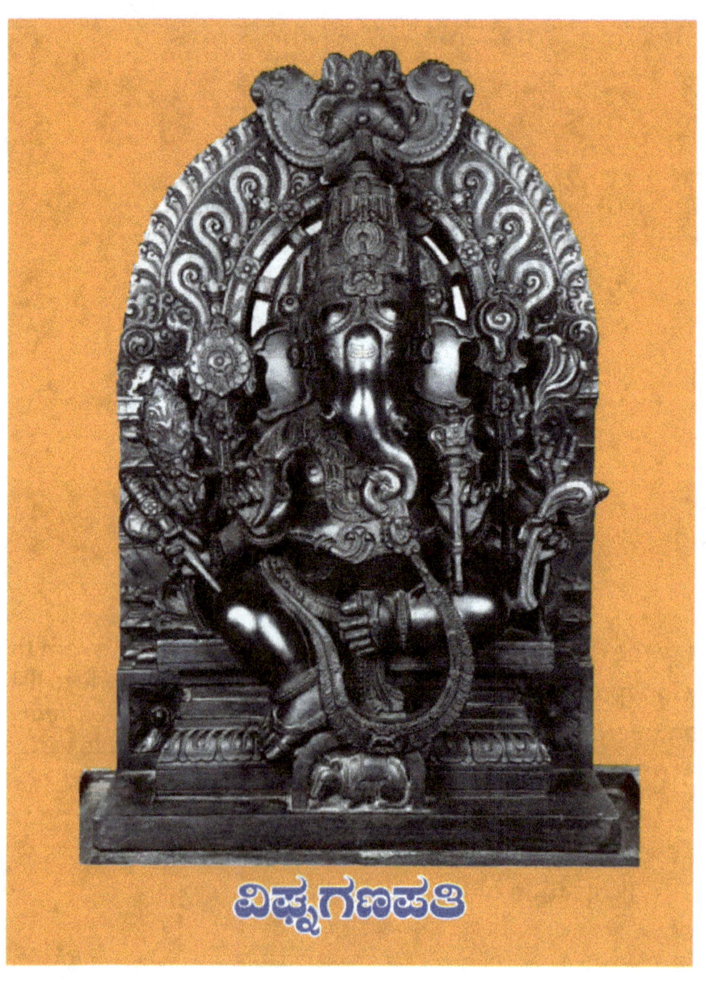

Suggested for those with the birth *nakshatra*
Rōhiṇī (रोहिणी)

09. ಶ್ರೀ ವಿಘ್ನ ಗಣಪತಿ (Śrī Vighna Gaṇapati)

https://flic.kr/p/89uMUY

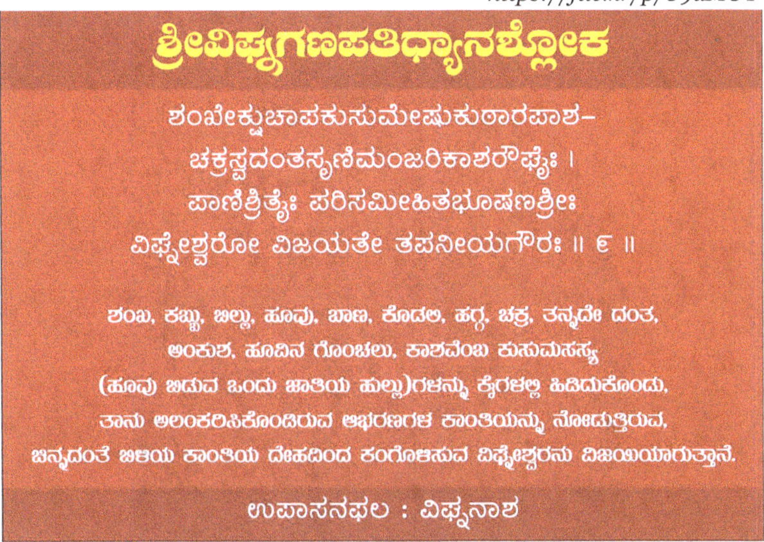

Śrī Vighna Gaṇapati dhyāna śloka

He, who bears conch, sugarcane, flowers, dagger, ripe, wheel, tusk, hook, bunch of tender leaves and *darbha* grass in His hands, and Who shines gloriously with the splendor of ornaments, the *Vighnēśvara*, the Essence of all Lights, is ever victorious

upāsana phala:
Destruction of Obstacles

Please scan this QR Code to listen to the *dhyāna śloka* in various languages of 🇮🇳

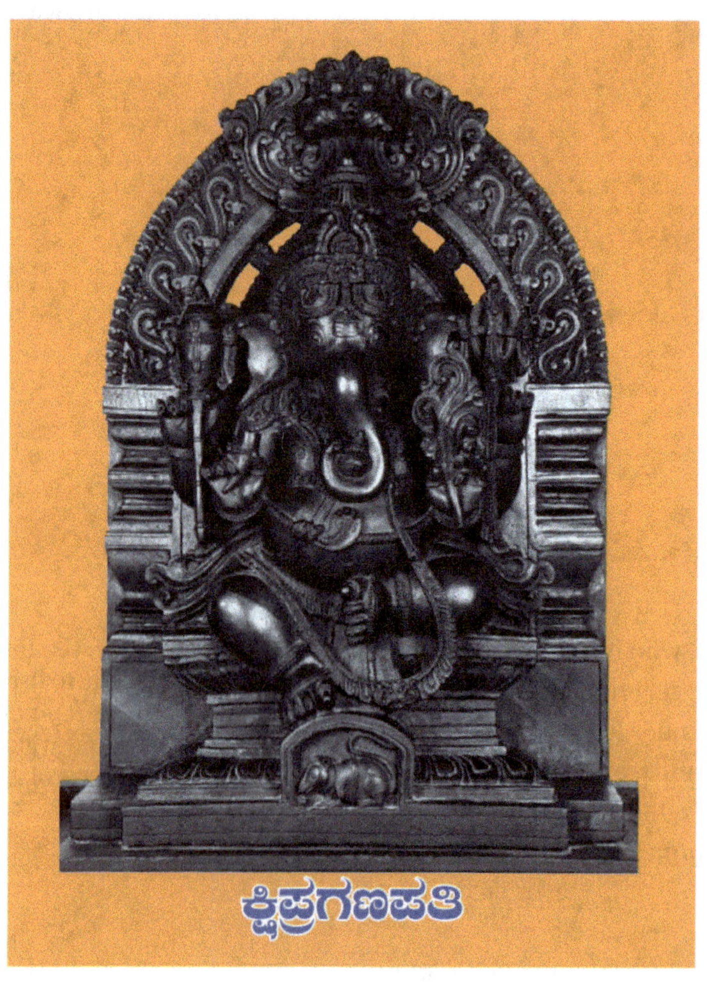

Suggested for those with the birth *nakshatra*
Mrigaśirā (मृगशिर)

10. ಶ್ರೀ ಕ್ಷಿಪ್ರ ಗಣಪತಿ (Śrī Kshipra Gaṇapati)

https://flic.kr/p/89uSnf

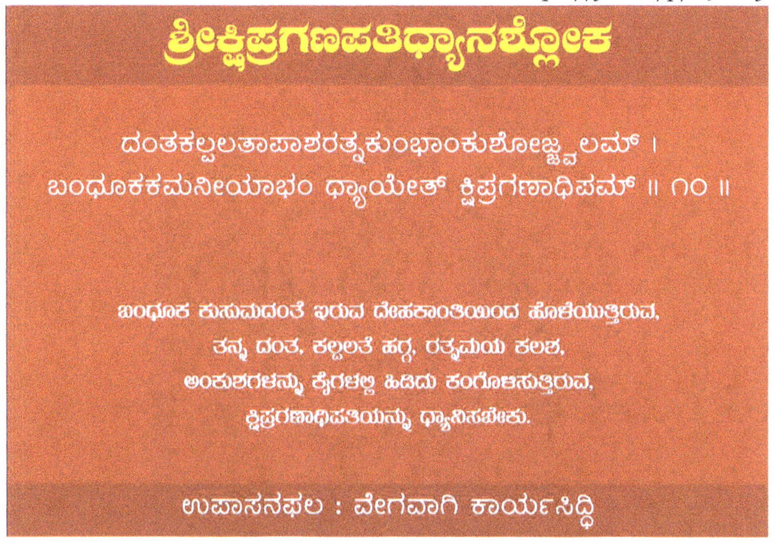

Śrī Kshipra Gaṇapati dhyāna śloka

I meditate on the effulgent *Kshipra Gaṇapati* with tusk, wish-yielding creeper, noose, bejeweled pot, and hook, and glowing brilliantly like the *bandhūka* flower

upāsana phala:
Fast Task Completion

Please scan this QR Code to listen to the *dhyāna śloka* in various languages of 🇮🇳

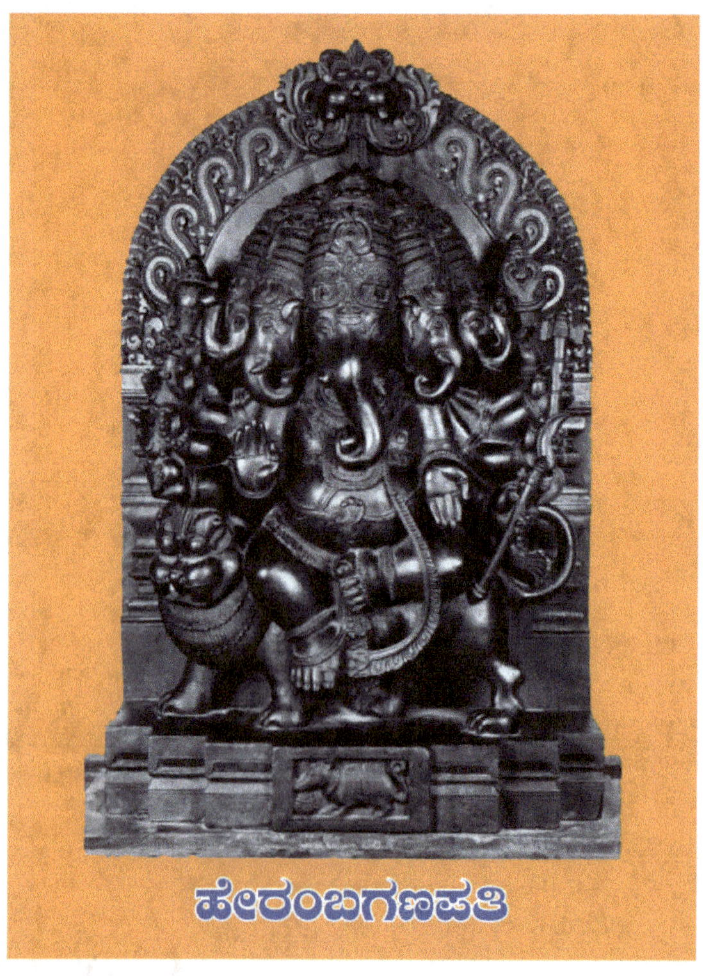

Suggested for those with the birth *nakshatra*
Ardra (आर्द्रा)

11. ಶ್ರೀ ಹೇರಂಬ ಗಣಪತಿ (Śrī Heramba Gaṇapati)

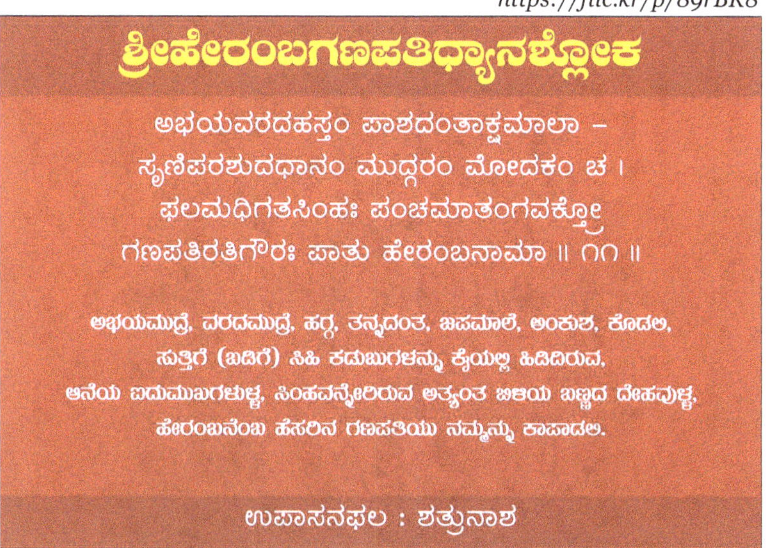

Śrī Heramba Gaṇapati dhyāna śloka

May *Heramba Gaṇapati* protect us, Who holds His (two) hands in gestures of protection and granting of boons and adorns in the other hands noose, tusk, rosary, hook, ax, hammer, sweets, and fruits riding a lion, having elephant faces and of snow-white color

upāsana phala:
Annihilation of Enemies

Please scan this QR Code to listen to the *dhyāna śloka* in various languages of 🇮🇳

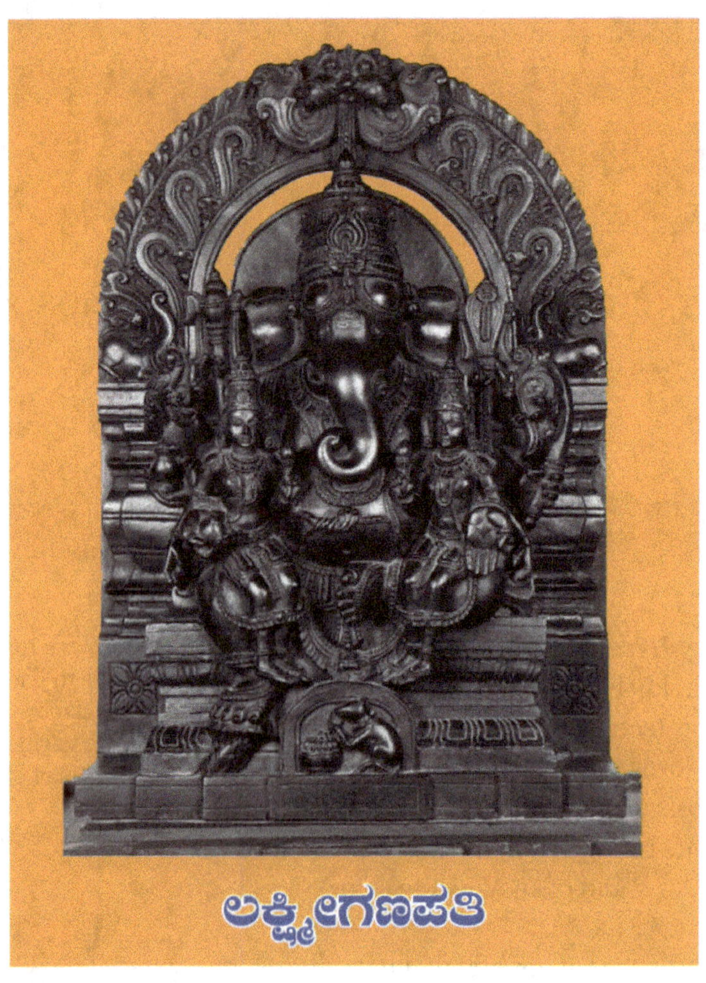

Suggested for those with the birth *nakshatra*
Punarvasu (पुनर्वसु)

12. ಶ್ರೀ ಲಕ್ಷ್ಮೀ ಗಣಪತಿ (Śrī Lakṣmī Gaṇapati)

https://flic.kr/p/89rBUi

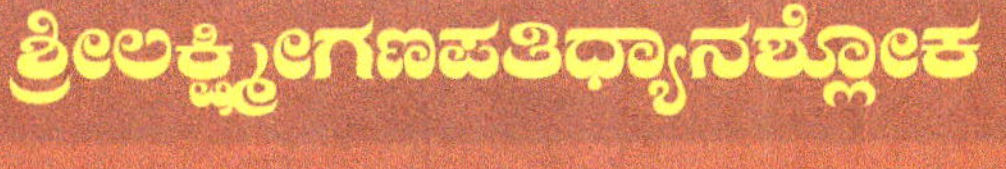

Śrī Lakṣmī Gaṇapati dhyāna śloka

May Lord *Lakṣmī Gaṇapati* Who is having in His hands parrot, apples, brilliant bejeweled pot, hook, noose, wish yielding creeper, sword and nectar, with two blue-lotus-bearing maidens serving, Him on both sides, fair complexioned and engrossed in the trumpet sound of the elephant, protect us

upāsana phala:
Prosperity

Please scan this QR Code to listen to the *dhyāna śloka* in various languages of 🇮🇳

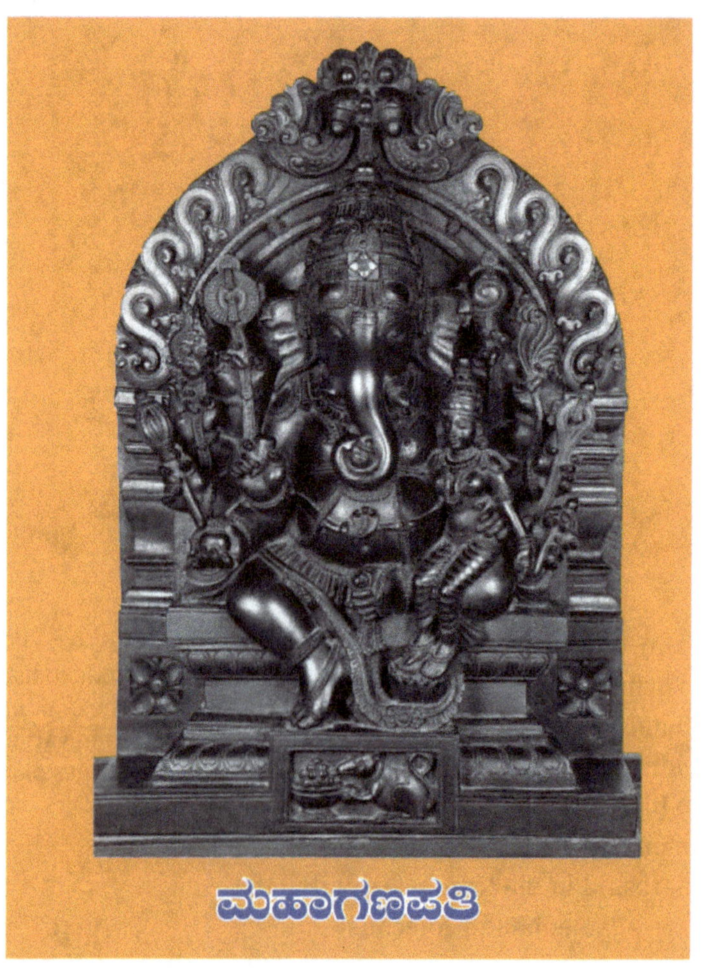

Suggested for those with the birth *nakshatra*
Pushya (पुष्य)

13. ಶ್ರೀ ಮಹಾ ಗಣಪತಿ (Śrī Mahā Gaṇapati)

https://flic.kr/p/89rBXH

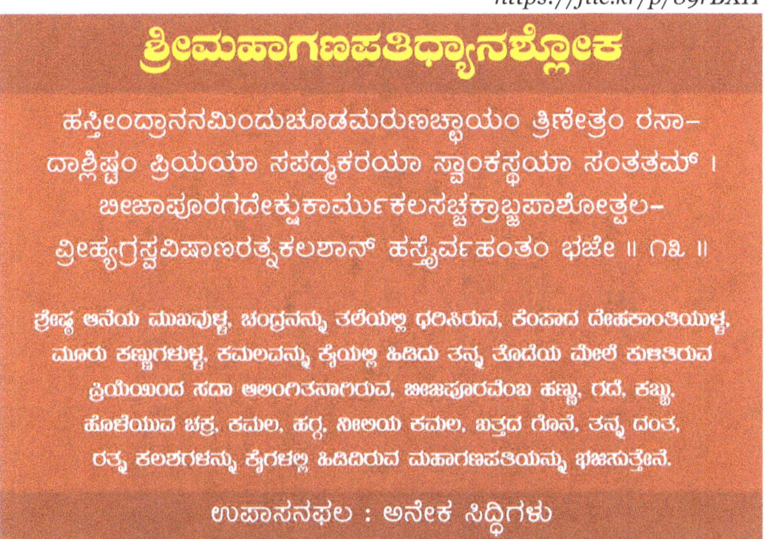

ಶ್ರೀಮಹಾಗಣಪತಿಧ್ಯಾನಶ್ಲೋಕ

ಹಸ್ತೀಂದ್ರಾನನಮಿಂದುಚೂಡಮರುಣಚ್ಛಾಯಂ ತ್ರಿಣೇತ್ರಂ ರಸಾ–
ದಾಶ್ಲಿಷ್ಟಂ ಪ್ರಿಯಯಾ ಸಪದ್ಮಕರಯಾ ಸ್ವಾಂಕಸ್ಥಯಾ ಸಂತತಮ್ ।
ಬೀಜಾಪೂರಗದೇಕ್ಷುಕಾರ್ಮುಕಲಸಚ್ಚಕ್ರಾಬ್ಜಪಾಶೋತ್ಪಲ–
ವ್ರೀಹ್ಯಗ್ರಸ್ವವಿಷಾಣರತ್ನಕಲಶಾನ್ ಹಸ್ತೈರ್ವಹಂತಂ ಭಜೇ ॥ ೧೩ ॥

ಶ್ರೇಷ್ಠ ಆನೆಯ ಮುಖವುಳ್ಳ, ಚಂದ್ರನನ್ನು ತಲೆಯಲ್ಲಿ ಧರಿಸಿರುವ, ಕೆಂಪಾದ ದೇಹಕಾಂತಿಯುಳ್ಳ,
ಮೂರು ಕಣ್ಣುಗಳುಳ್ಳ, ಕಮಲವನ್ನು ಕೈಯಲ್ಲಿ ಹಿಡಿದು ತನ್ನ ತೊಡೆಯ ಮೇಲೆ ಕುಳಿತಿರುವ
ಪ್ರಿಯೆಯಿಂದ ಸದಾ ಆಲಿಂಗಿತನಾಗಿರುವ, ಬೀಜಪೂರವೆಂಬ ಹಣ್ಣು, ಗದೆ, ಕಬ್ಬು,
ಹೊಳೆಯುವ ಚಕ್ರ, ಕಮಲ, ಹಗ್ಗ, ನೀಲಿಯ ಕಮಲ, ಖತ್ತದ ಗೊನೆ, ತನ್ನ ದಂತ,
ರತ್ನ ಕಲಶಗಳನ್ನು ಕೈಗಳಲ್ಲಿ ಹಿಡಿದಿರುವ ಮಹಾಗಣಪತಿಯನ್ನು ಭಜಿಸುತ್ತೇನೆ.

ಉಪಾಸನಫಲ : ಅನೇಕ ಸಿದ್ಧಿಗಳು

Śrī Mahā Gaṇapati dhyāna śloka

I worship Lord *Mahā Gaṇapati* who is having the face of the divine elephant bedecked with the crescent on His head, red in complexion, three-eyed, embracing His beloved consort with a lotus in her hand and who dwells ever in Her heart, Who in His hands holds pomegranate, sugarcane, bow, effulgent wheel, lotus, lilies, paddy, corn ears, own (broken) tusk, and bejeweled pot

upāsana phala:
Many abilities/powers

Please scan this QR Code to listen to the *dhyāna śloka* in various languages of 🇮🇳

Āśleṣā (आश्लेषा/आश्लेषा)

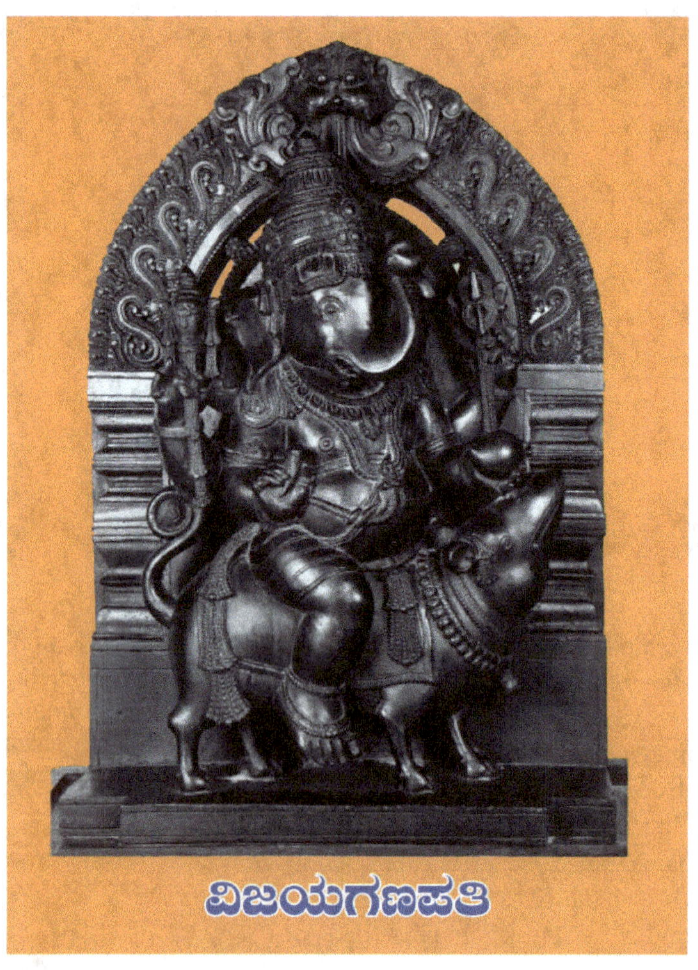

Suggested for those with the birth *nakshatra*
Āśleṣā (आश्लेषा/आश्लेषा)

14. ಶ್ರೀ ವಿಜಯ ಗಣಪತಿ (Śrī Vijaya Gaṇapati)

https://flic.kr/p/89uSyj

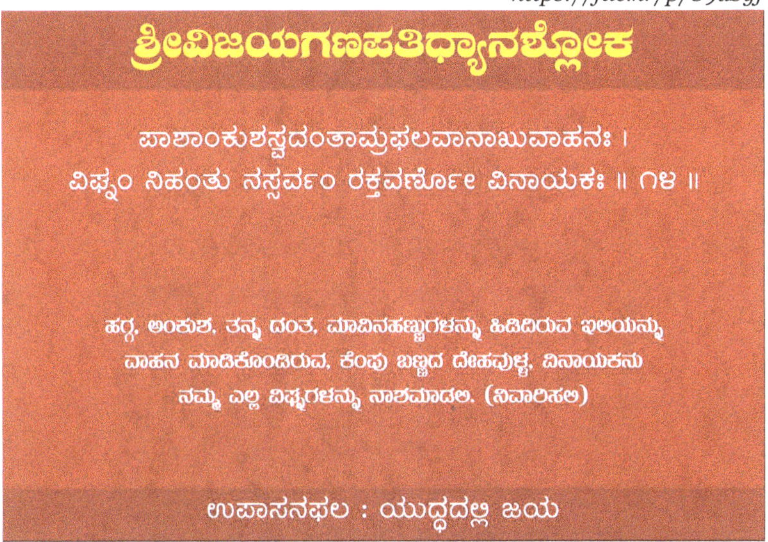

Śrī Vijaya Gaṇapati dhyāna śloka

I meditate on Lord *Vijaya Gaṇapati* red in complexion, the destroyer of all obstacles, riding His vehicle the mouse, and who carries noose, hook tusk, and fruits in His hands

upāsana phala:
Victory in War

Please scan this QR Code to listen to the *dhyāna śloka* in various languages of 🇮🇳

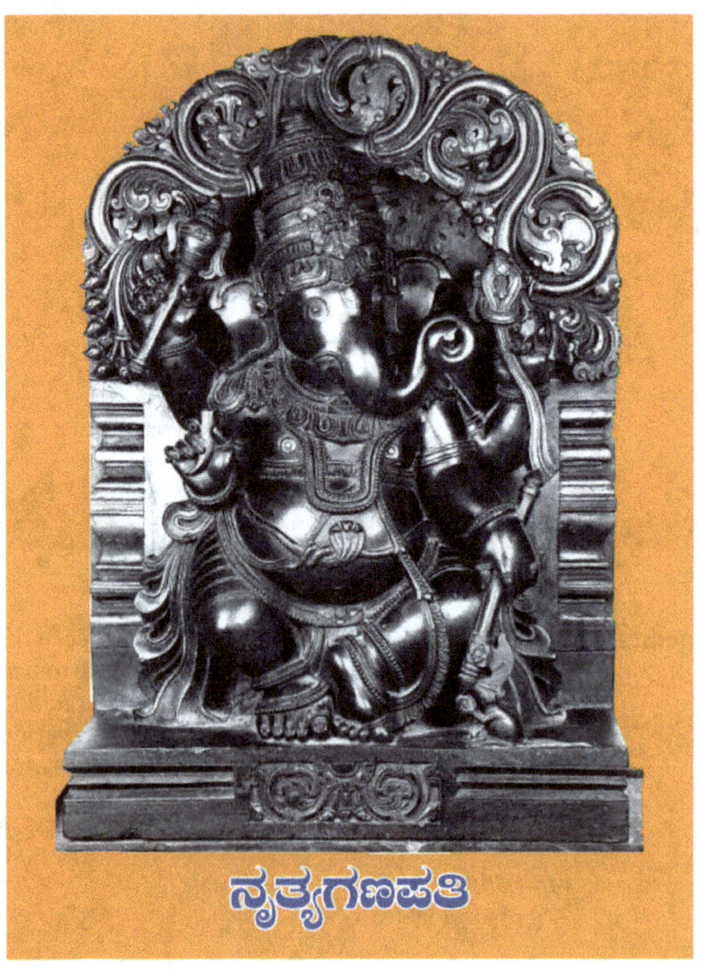

Suggested for those with the birth *nakshatra*
Maghā (मघा)

15. ಶ್ರೀ ನೃತ್ಯ ಗಣಪತಿ (Śrī Nṛtya Gaṇapati)

https://flic.kr/p/89rC2D

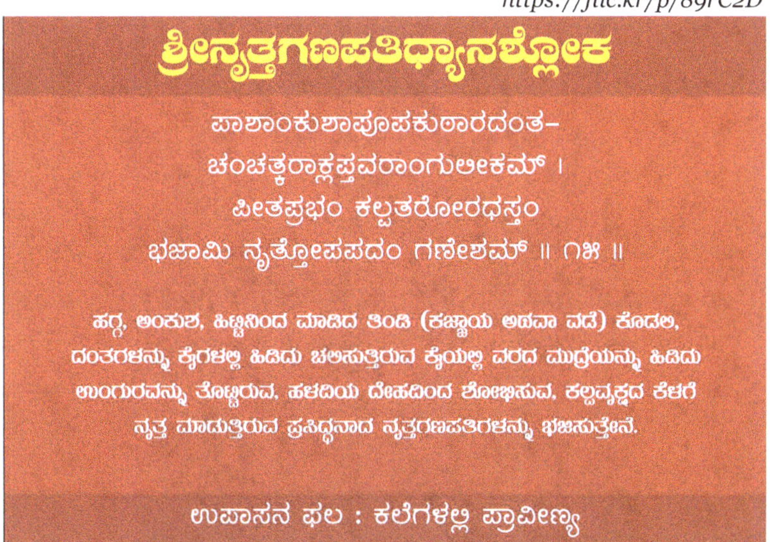

Śrī Nṛtya Gaṇapati dhyāna śloka

I worship Lord *Nṛtya Gaṇapati* (the dancing Lord) Who is holding in His hands noose, hook, cake, dagger and tusk, Who adorns divine rings in His delicate fingers, Whose hands sway (in dance) in Whose (one) hand is a tusk, and who glows with His golden-hued belly

upāsana phala:
Proficiency in the Arts

Please scan this QR Code to listen to the *dhyāna śloka* in various languages of 🇮🇳

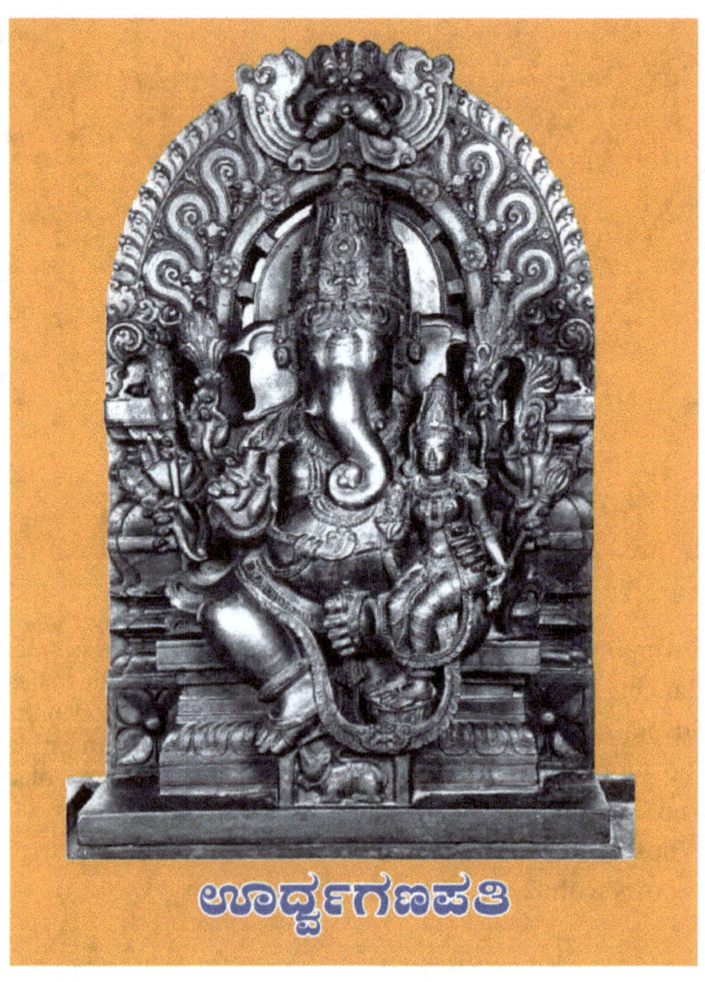

Suggested for those with the birth *nakshatra*
Pūrva Phālguṇī (पूर्व फाल्गुनी)

16. ಶ್ರೀ ಊರ್ಧ್ವ ಗಣಪತಿ (Śrī Ūrdhva Gaṇapati)

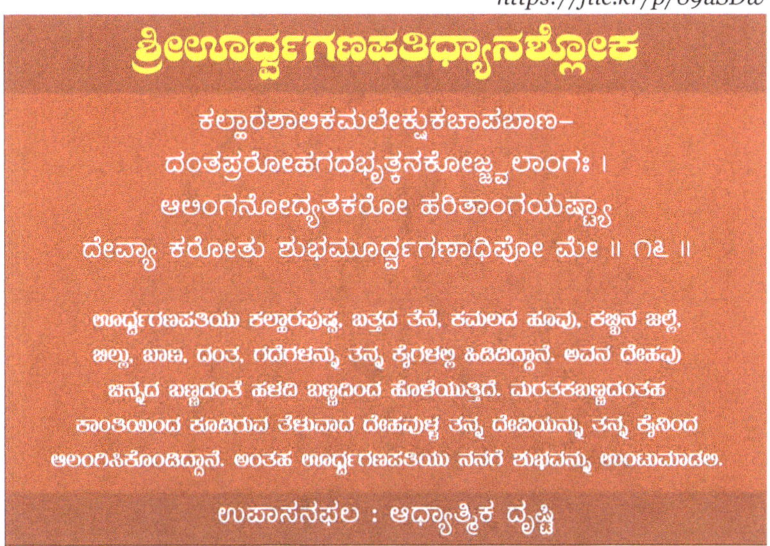

Śrī Ūrdhva Gaṇapati dhyāna śloka

May Lord *Ūrdhva Gaṇapati*, Who is decorated with flowers, corn-ears, lotus, sugarcane, bow and arrow, tusk, tender grass sprout, and mace and Whose body shines like gold, Who lifts His hands to embrace the green complexioned Devi, bless me with auspiciousness

upāsana phala:
Focus on Spirituality

Please scan this QR Code to listen to the *dhyāna śloka* in various languages of 🇮🇳

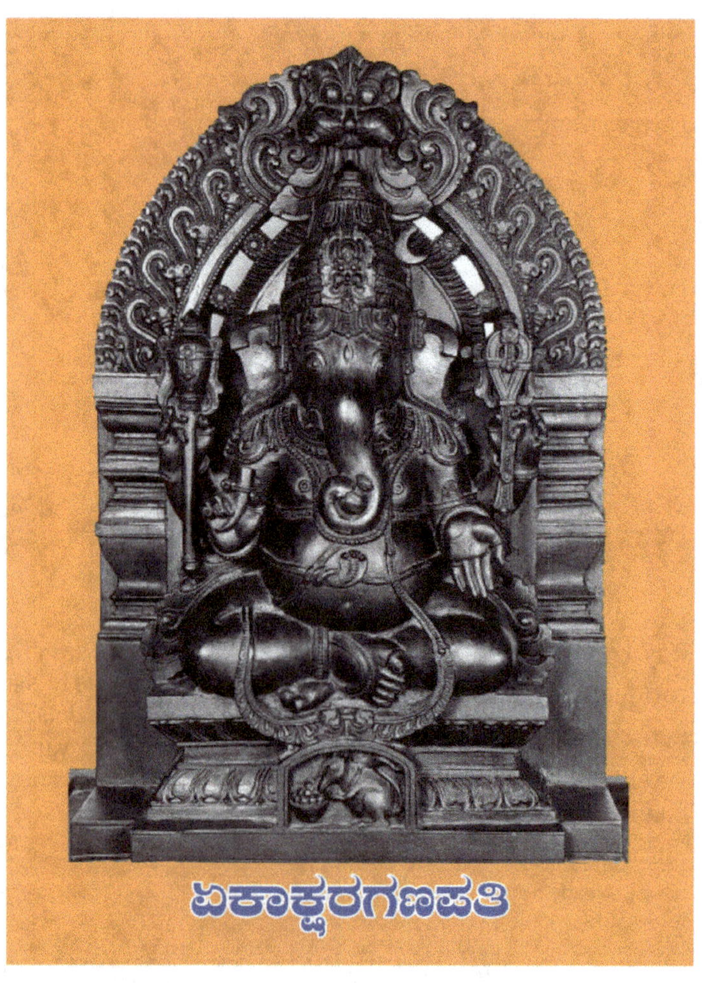

Suggested for those with the birth *nakshatra*
Uttara Phālguṇī (उत्तर फाल्गुनी)

17. ಶ್ರೀ ಏಕಾಕ್ಷರ ಗಣಪತಿ (Śrī Ekākshara Gaṇapati)

https://flic.kr/p/89rC9x

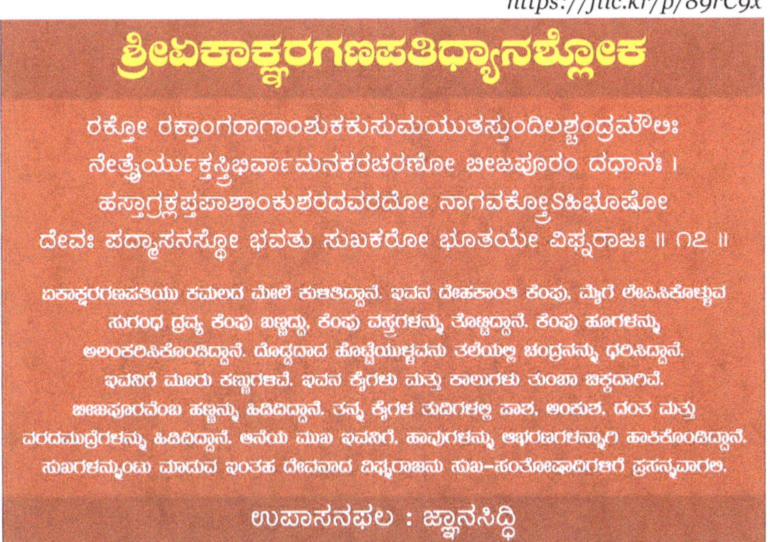

Śrī Ekākshara Gaṇapati dhyāna śloka

May Lord *Ekākshara Gaṇapati* bestow happiness on us, Who is the destroyer of obstacles, Who is of red complexion, wielding a red-hook, holding a flower, pot-bellied, decorated with crescent in His locks, possessing three eyes and short limbs, with guava fruit in one hand and noose, hook and tusk in other hands, who is the bestower of boons, elephant-faced and wearing serpents as ornaments and who is seated in lotus posture (*padmāsana*)

upāsana phala:
Gaining *Jñāna*

Please scan this QR Code to listen to the *dhyāna śloka* in various languages of 🇮🇳

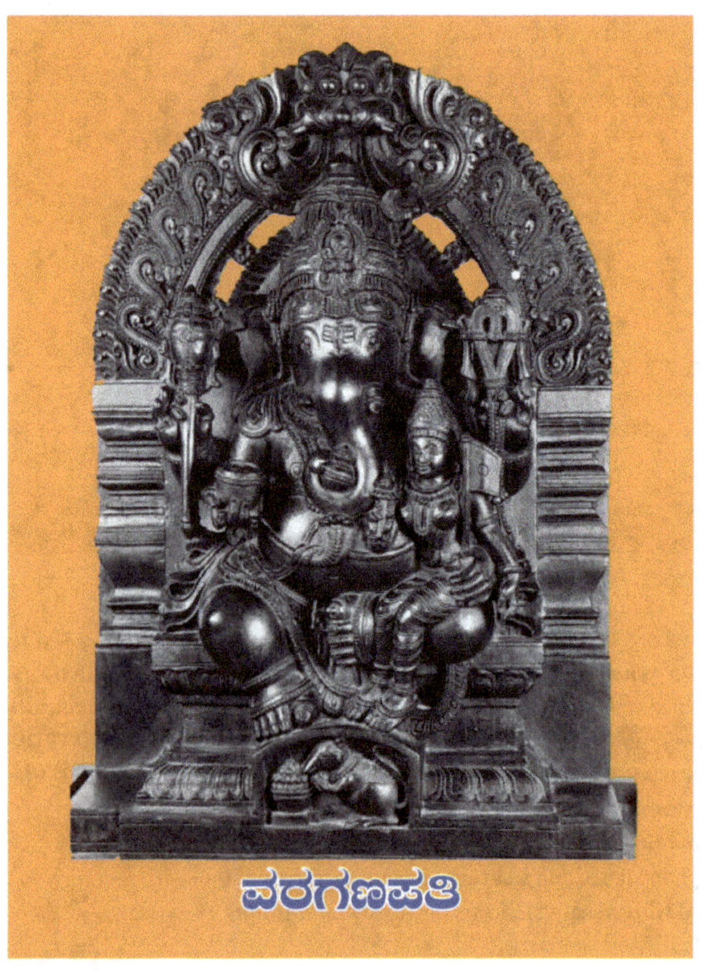

Suggested for those with the birth *nakshatra*
Hasta (हस्त)

18. ಶ್ರೀ ವರ ಗಣಪತಿ (*Śrī Vara Gaṇapati*)

ಶ್ರೀವರಗಣಪತಿಧ್ಯಾನಶ್ಲೋಕ

ಸಿಂಧೂರಾಭಮಿಭಾನನಂ ತ್ರಿಣಯನಂ ಹಸ್ತೇ ಚ ಪಾಶಾಂಕುಶೌ
ಬಿಭ್ರಾಣಂ ಮಧುಮತ್ಕಪಾಲಮನಿಶಂ ಸಾದ್ವಿಂದುಮೌಲಿಂ ಭಜೇ ॥
ಪುಷ್ಟ್ಯಾಶ್ಲಿಷ್ಟತನುಂ ದ್ವಜಾಗ್ರಕರಯಾ ಪದ್ಮೋಲ್ಲಸದ್ಧಸ್ತಯಾ
ತದ್ಯೋನ್ಯಾಹಿತಪಾಣಿಮಾತ್ತವಸುಮತ್ವಾತೋಲ್ಲಸತ್ಪುಷ್ಕರಮ್ ॥ ೧೮ ॥

ಸಿಂಧೂರದಂತಹ ಬಣ್ಣದ ಮುಖವುಳ್ಳ, ಮೂರು ಕಣ್ಣುಗಳುಳ್ಳ, ತನ್ನೆರಡು ಕೈಗಳಲ್ಲಿ ಪಾಶ ಮತ್ತು
ಅಂಕುಶಗಳನ್ನು ಹಿಡಿದಿರುವ, ಐನ್ನೆರಡು ಕೈಗಳಲ್ಲಿ ಮಧ್ಯ ತುಂಬಿದ ಕಪಾಲಗಳನ್ನುಳ್ಳ,
ಹೊಳೆಯುವ ಚಂದ್ರನನ್ನು ತಲೆಯಲ್ಲಿ ಧರಿಸಿರುವ, ವರಗಣಪತಿಯನ್ನು ಸದಾ ಭಜಿಸುತ್ತೇನೆ.
ಇವನ ಸಂಗಾತಿಯಾದ ಪುಷ್ಟಿದೇವಿಯು ಇವನನ್ನು ತನ್ನ ಒಂದು ಕೈಯಿಂದ ಆಲಂಗಿಸಿಕೊಂಡಿದ್ದಾಳೆ.
ಇನ್ನೊಂದು ಕೈಯಿಂದ ಕಮಲವನ್ನು ಹಿಡಿದುಕೊಂಡು ಕಂಗೊಳಿಸುತ್ತಿದ್ದಾಳೆ.
ಈ ದೇವನು ತನ್ನ ಸೊಂಡಿಲಿನಿಂದ ಸಂಪದ್ಧರಿತ ಪಾತ್ರೆಯನ್ನು ಹಿಡಿದುಕೊಂಡಿದ್ದಾನೆ.
ಉಪಾಸನಫಲ : ಕೋರಿದ ವರಗಳು

Śrī Vara Gaṇapati dhyāna śloka

I worship *Śrī Vara Gaṇapati* glowing like vermilion having elephant face, three eyes, wielding noose and hook (in two hands), with a honey-pot on his hands, decked with a crescent moon on His head, embracing His lotus-and-flag-carrying consort *PushṭiDēvi* affectionately

upāsana phala:
Requested Boons

Please scan this QR Code to listen to the *dhyāna śloka* in various languages of 🇮🇳

ॐ *Swānanda*

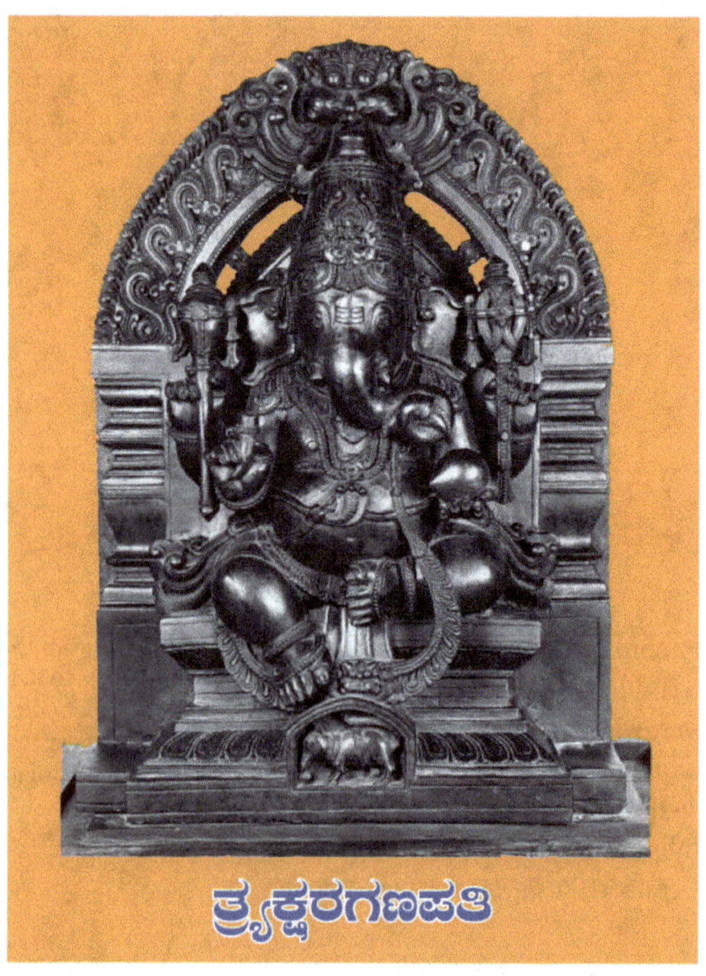

Suggested for those with the birth *nakshatra*
Chitrā (चित्रा)

19. ಶ್ರೀ ತ್ರ್ಯಕ್ಷರ ಗಣಪತಿ (Śrī Tryakshara Gaṇapati)

https://flic.kr/p/89rCWM

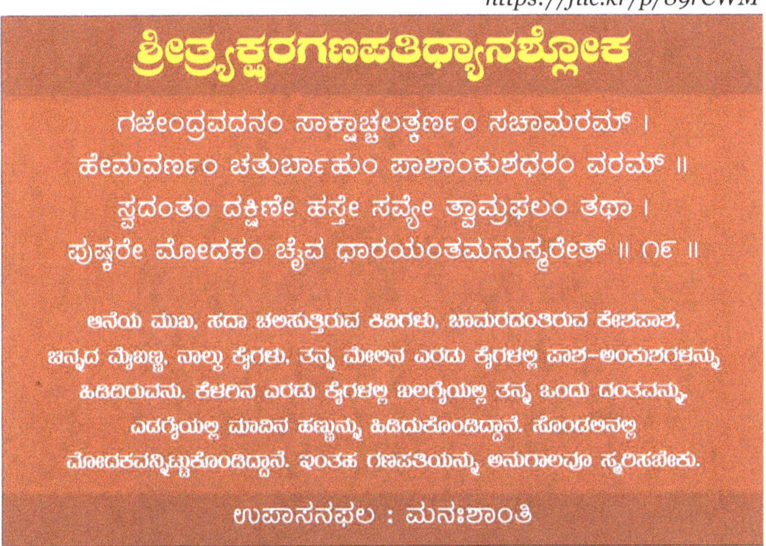

Śrī Tryakshara Gaṇapati dhyāna śloka

One should remember the three-eyed *Lord Tryakshara Gaṇapati*, Whose elephant face glitters like gold, Who is the bestower of boons, Who is four-armed, carrying noose, hook, lotus and sweet in His hands, His own (broken) tusk in the right hand and mango in the left hand

upāsana phala:
Peace of Mind

Please scan this QR Code to listen to the *dhyāna śloka* in various languages of 🇮🇳

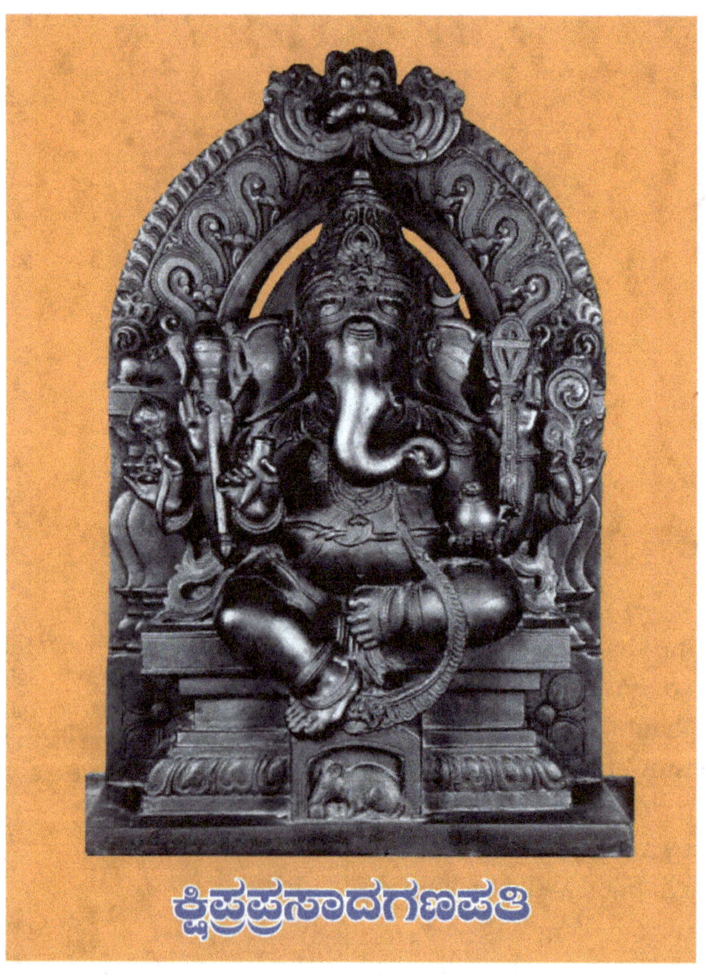

Suggested for those with the birth *nakshatra*
Svāti (स्वाति)

20. ಶ್ರೀ ಕ್ಷಿಪ್ರಪ್ರಸಾದ ಗಣಪತಿ (Śrī KshipraPrasāda Gaṇapati)

https://flic.kr/p/89uTBU

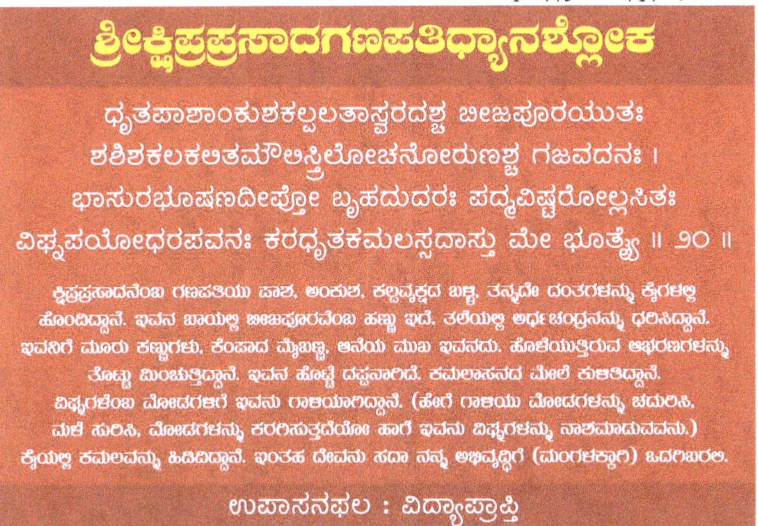

Śrī KshipraPrasāda Gaṇapati dhyāna śloka

May Lord *KshipraPrasāda Gaṇapati*, adorned with noose, hook, wish-yielding creeper, tusk and apple, Who sports a crown decked with the crescent, three-eyed, elephant faced, red-complexioned and decorated with shining ornaments and pot-bellied, Who makes the lotus (in His hands) dance in His breath and Who wields a club to destroy the clouds of obstacles, shower prosperity upon me

upāsana phala:
Education

Please scan this QR Code to listen to the *dhyāna śloka* in various languages of 🇮🇳

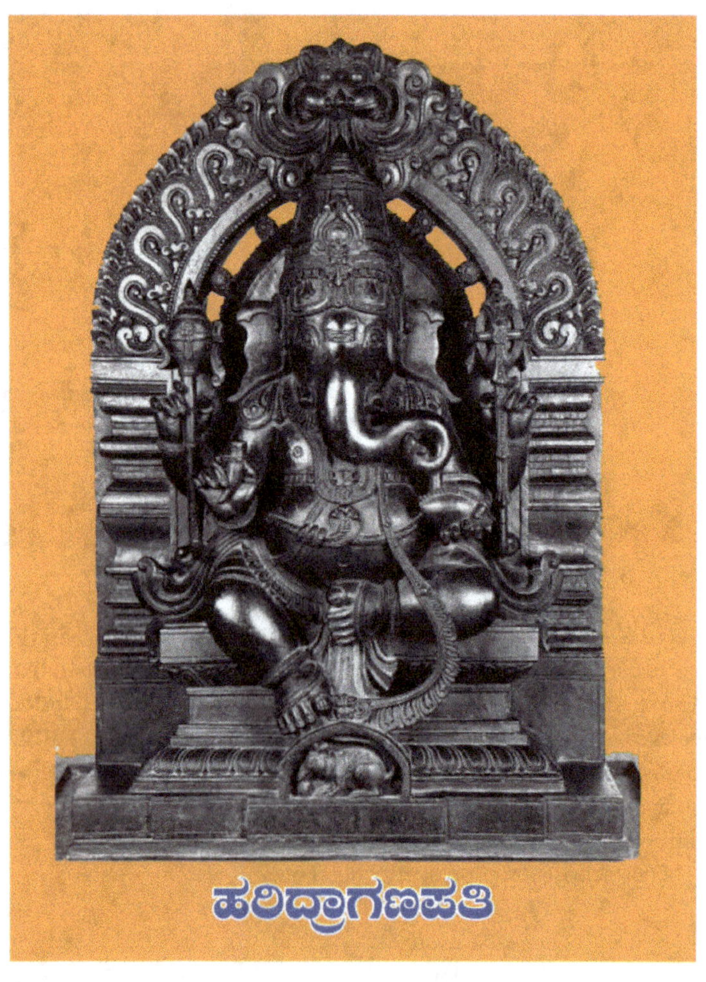

Suggested for those with the birth *nakshatra*
Viśākhā (विशाखा)

21. ಶ್ರೀ ಹರಿದ್ರಾ ಗಣಪತಿ (Śrī Haridrā Gaṇapati)

https://flic.kr/p/89uTEh

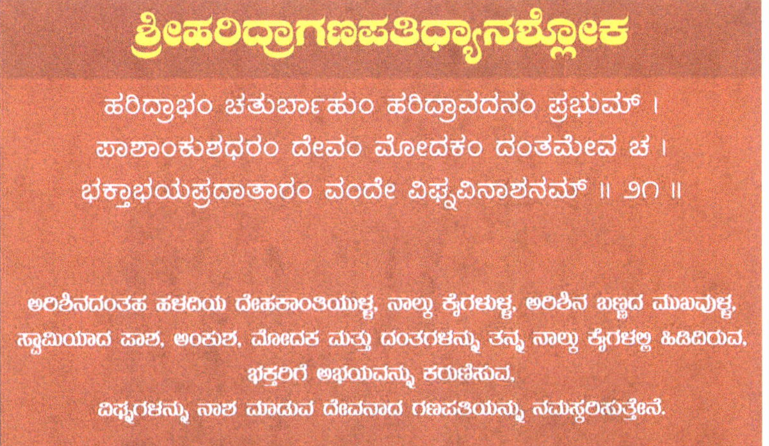

Śrī Haridrā Gaṇapati dhyāna śloka

I salute Lord *Haridrā Gaṇapati*, Who is radiant like turmeric yellow, Whose face shines with yellow complexion, Who has four hands (three) carrying noose, hook, and sweetmeat and the (fourth) giving complete refuge to His devotees, destroying all their fears

upāsana phala:
Accomplishment of Good Tasks

Please scan this QR Code to listen to the *dhyāna śloka* in various languages of 🇮🇳

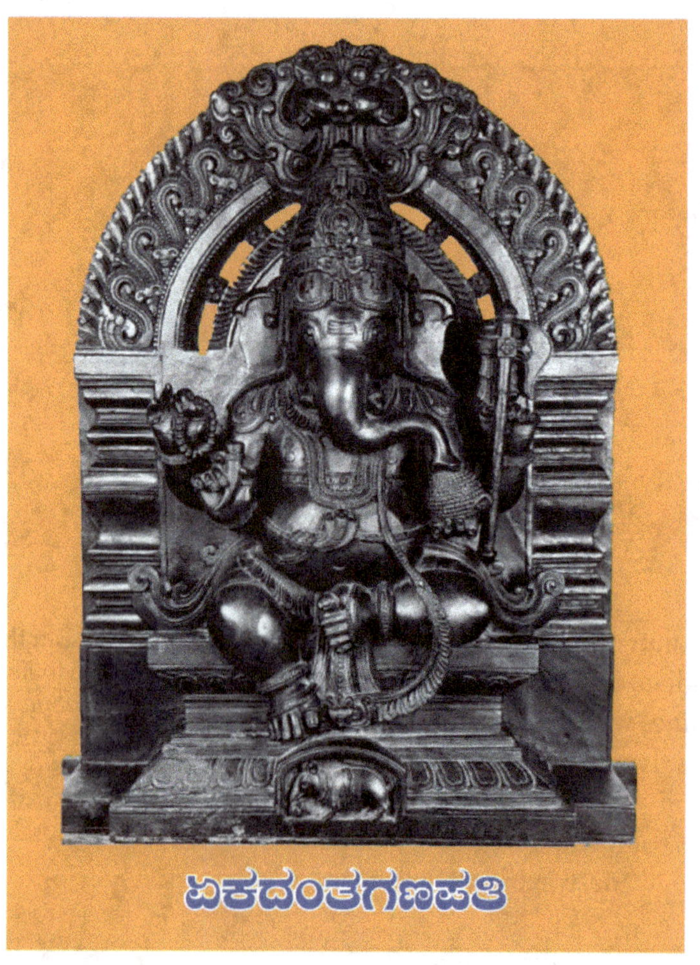

Suggested for those with the birth *nakshatra*
Anurādha (अनुराधा)

22. ಶ್ರೀ ಏಕದಂತ ಗಣಪತಿ (Śrī Ekadanta Gaṇapati)

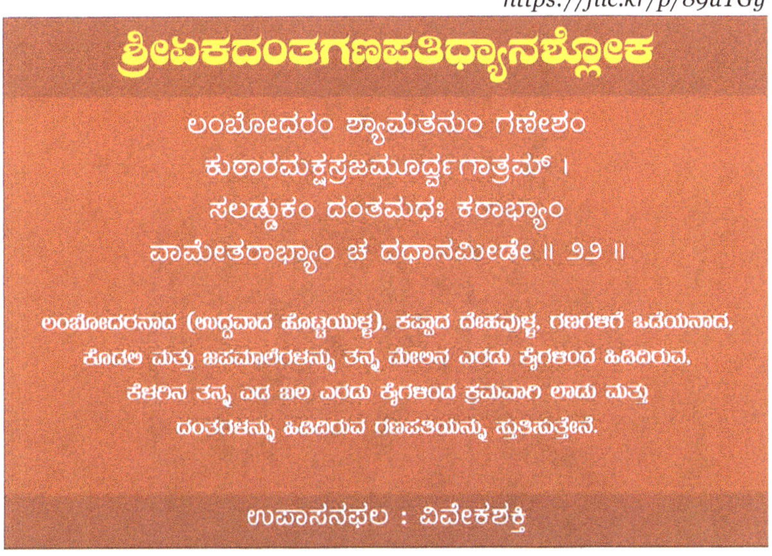

Śrī Ekadanta Gaṇapati dhyāna śloka

I invoke the pot-bellied, dark-complexioned, Lord *Ekadanta Gaṇapati*, Who sports an ax, sugarcane, rosary, *laḍḍu*, and tusk in His hands

upāsana phala:
Power of Discernment

Please scan this QR Code to listen to the *dhyāna śloka* in various languages of 🇮🇳

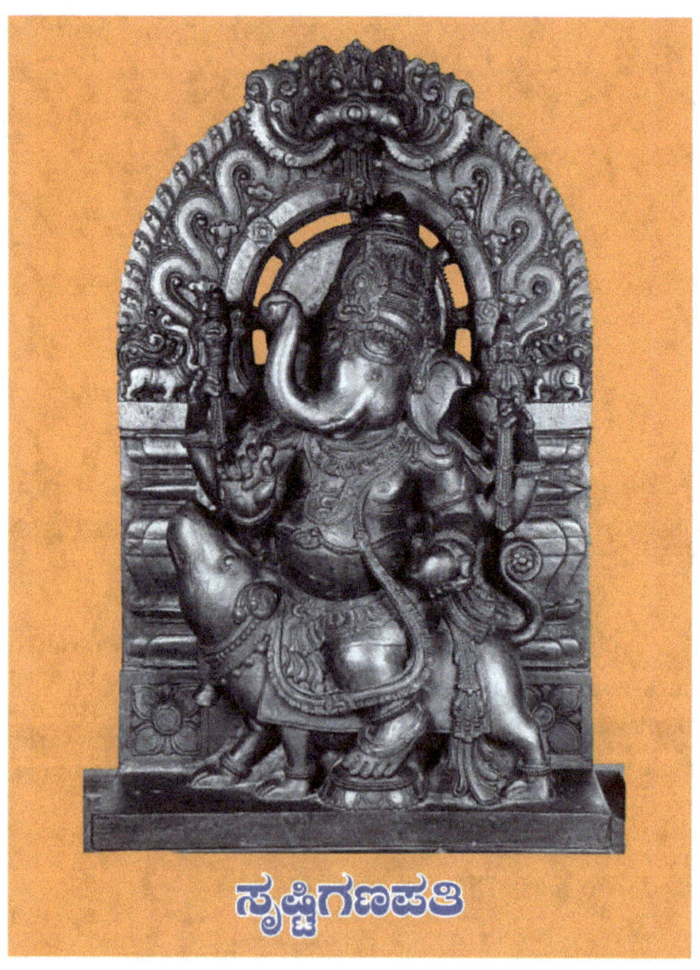

Suggested for those with the birth *nakshatra*
Jyeṣṭā (ज्येष्ठा)

23. ಶ್ರೀ ಸೃಷ್ಟಿ ಗಣಪತಿ (Śrī Sṛishṭi Gaṇapati)

https://flic.kr/p/89rD6F

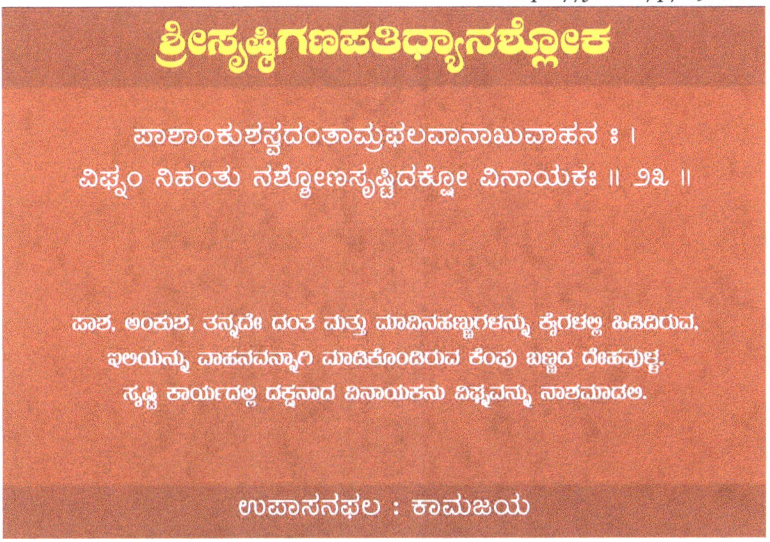

Śrī Sṛishṭi Gaṇapati dhyāna śloka

May Lord *Vināyaka*, adorning noose, hook, tusk and mango in His hands sitting on His vehicle, the mouse, red-complexioned and Who is efficient in His creation, remove all obstacles and protect us

upāsana phala:
Victory over Lust

Please scan this QR Code to listen to the *dhyāna śloka* in various languages of 🇮🇳

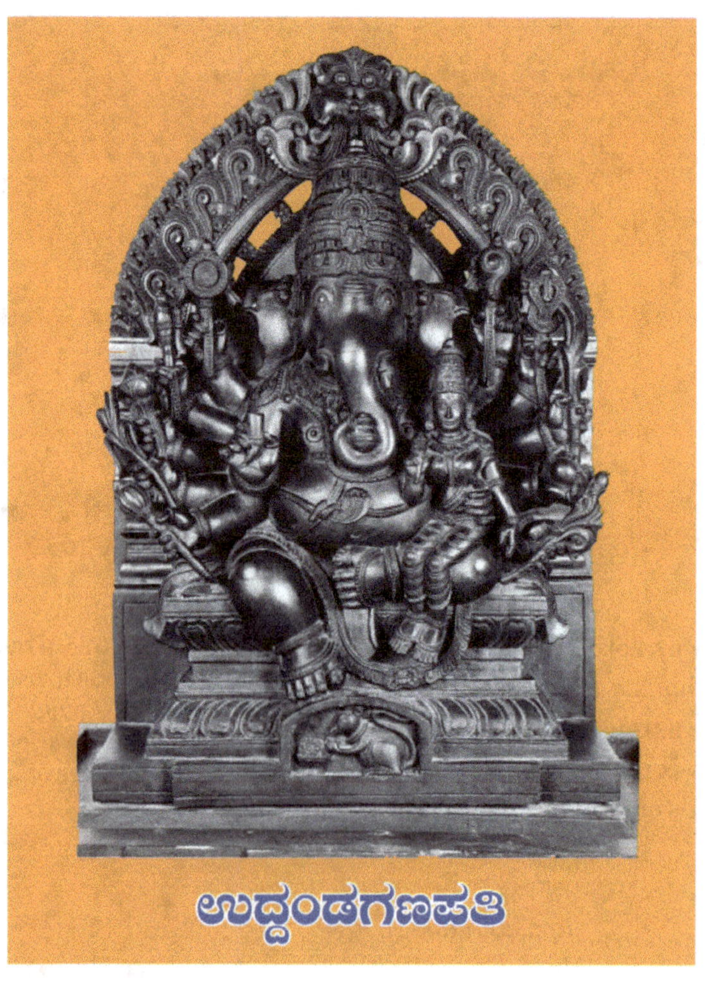

Suggested for those with the birth *nakshatra*
Mūla (मूल)

24. ಶ್ರೀ ಉದ್ದಂಡ ಗಣಪತಿ (Śrī Uddaṇḍa Gaṇapati)

https://flic.kr/p/89rD9v

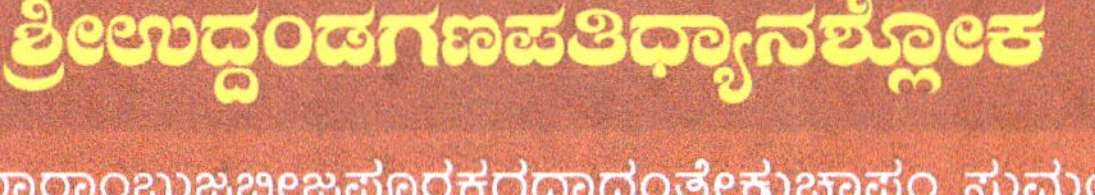

Śrī Uddaṇḍa Gaṇapati dhyāna śloka

May *Uddaṇḍa Gaṇapati*, having red complexion, sporting red lily, guava, mace, tusk, sugarcane, arrow, flower, paddy corn-ear, pot and noose in His multiple hands, embracing His fair-complexioned consort, bestow auspiciousness on us

upāsana phala:
Better Ability than Others

Please scan this QR Code to listen to the *dhyāna śloka* in various languages of 🇮🇳

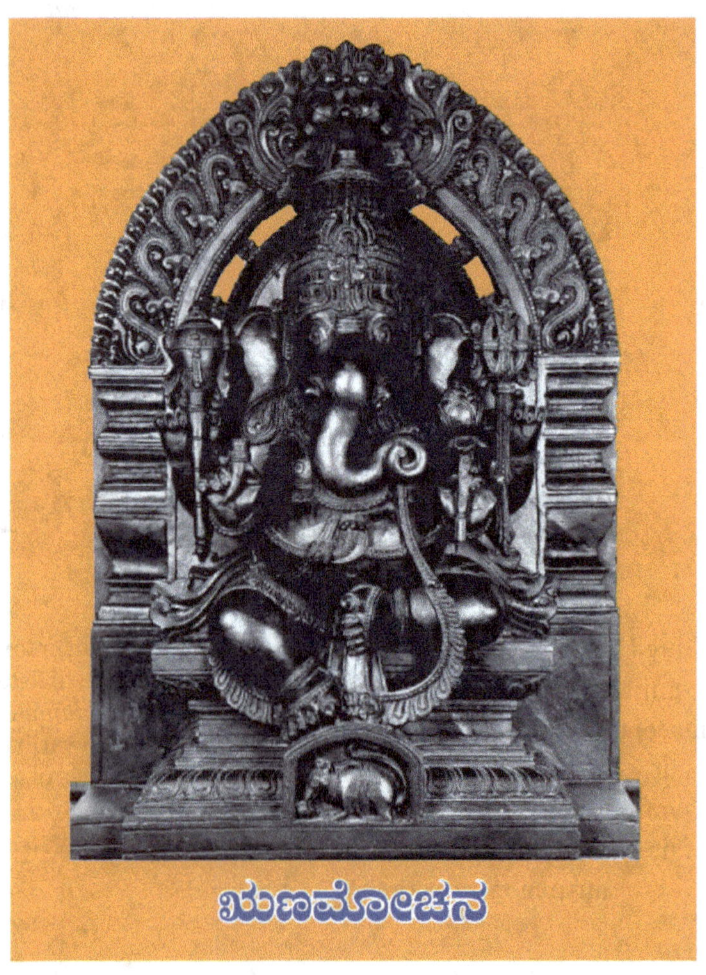

Suggested for those with the birth *nakshatra*
Pūrva Āṣāḍā (पूर्व आषाढ)

25. ಶ್ರೀ ಋಣಮೋಚನ ಗಣಪತಿ (Śrī R̥iṇamochana Gaṇapati)

https://flic.kr/p/89uTPm

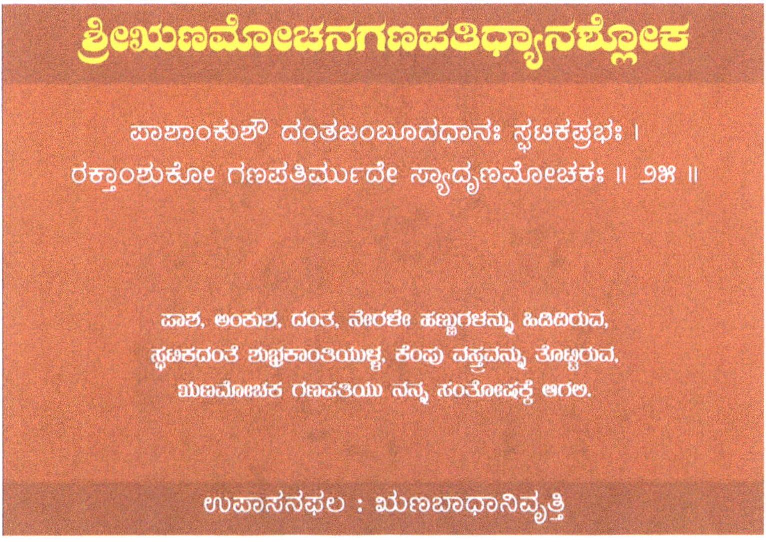

Śrī R̥iṇamochana Gaṇapati dhyāna śloka

May Lord R̥iṇamochana Gaṇapati, holding noose, hook, tusk, and rose apple in His hands, shining like a crystal, and adorning red clothes liberate us from all our debts (liabilities) and bestow happiness on us

upāsana phala:
Liberation from the Pain of Burdens

Please scan this QR Code to listen to the *dhyāna śloka* in various languages of 🇮🇳

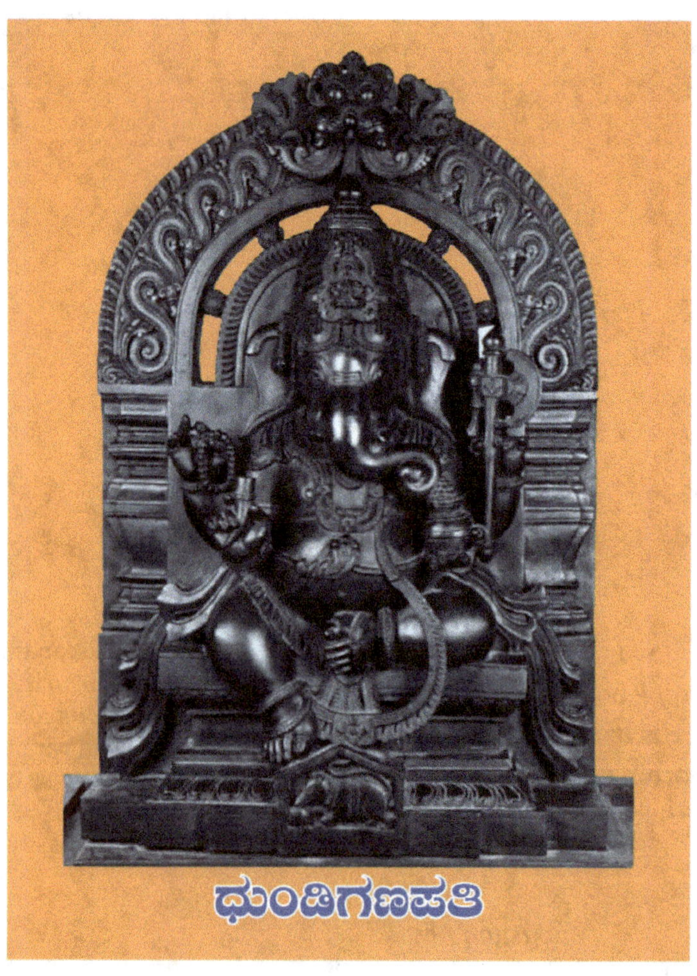

Suggested for those with the birth *nakshatra*
Uttara Āṣāḍā (उत्तर आषाढा)

26. ಶ್ರೀ ಧುಂಡಿ ಗಣಪತಿ (Śrī Dhuṇḍi Gaṇapati)

https://flic.kr/p/89uTQU

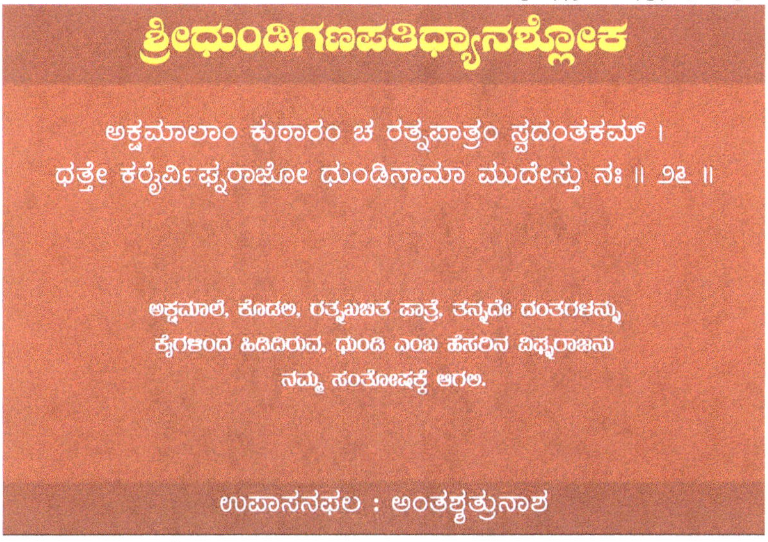

Śrī Dhuṇḍi Gaṇapati dhyāna śloka

May *Dhuṇḍi Gaṇapati*, having rosary, ax, bejeweled pot, and tusk in His hands bring eternal joy to us

upāsana phala:
Destruction of Internal Foes

Please scan this QR Code to listen to the *dhyāna śloka* in various languages of 🇮🇳

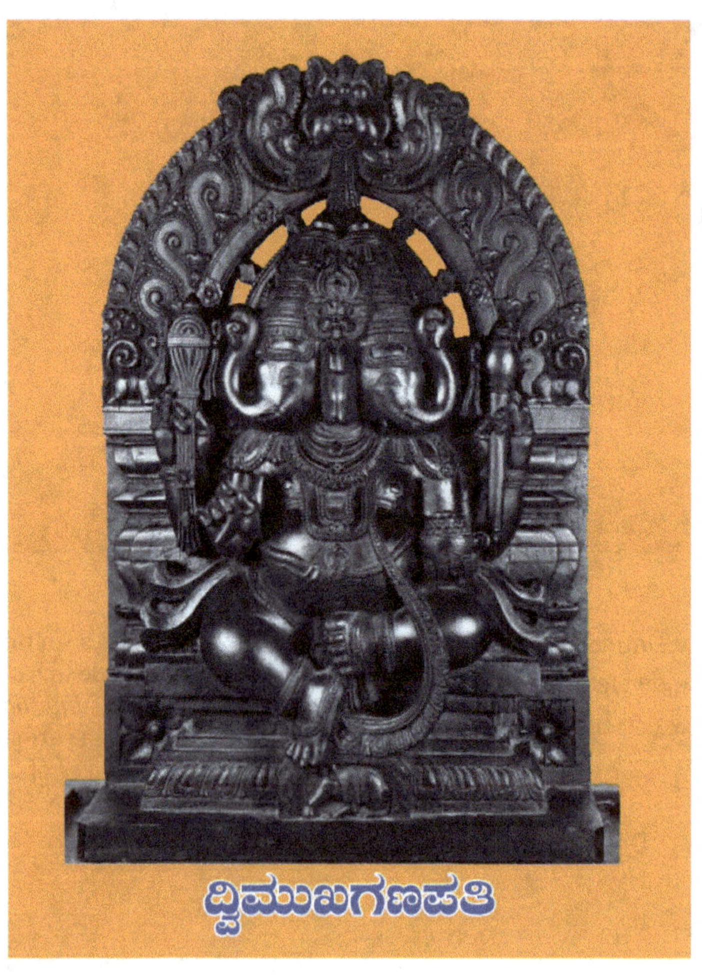

Suggested for those with the birth *nakshatra*
Śravaṇa (श्रवण)

27. ಶ್ರೀ ದ್ವಿಮುಖ ಗಣಪತಿ (Śrī Dvimukha Gaṇapati)

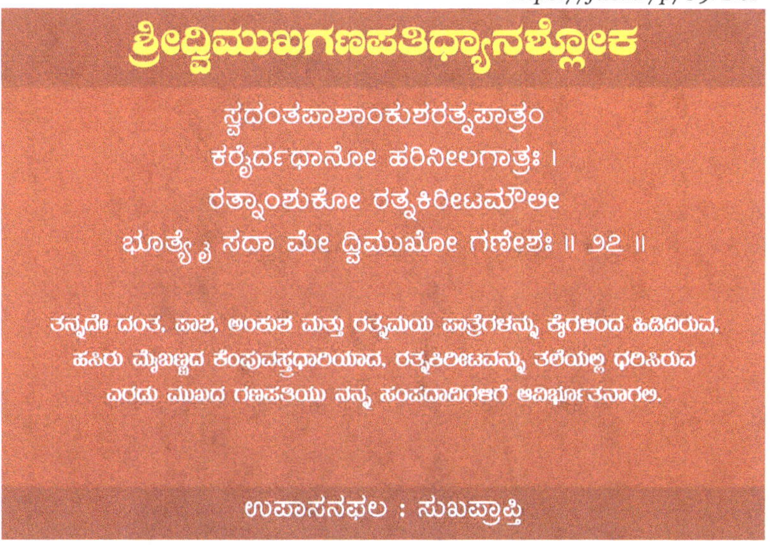

Śrī Dvimukha Gaṇapati dhyāna śloka

May the two-headed Lord *Gaṇapati* , holding tusk, noose, hook, and bejeweled pot in His hands, dark-complexioned, adorning red clothes, red crown and a garland be the precursor of my prosperity

upāsana phala:
Obtaining Bliss

Please scan this QR Code to listen to the *dhyāna śloka* in various languages of 🇮🇳

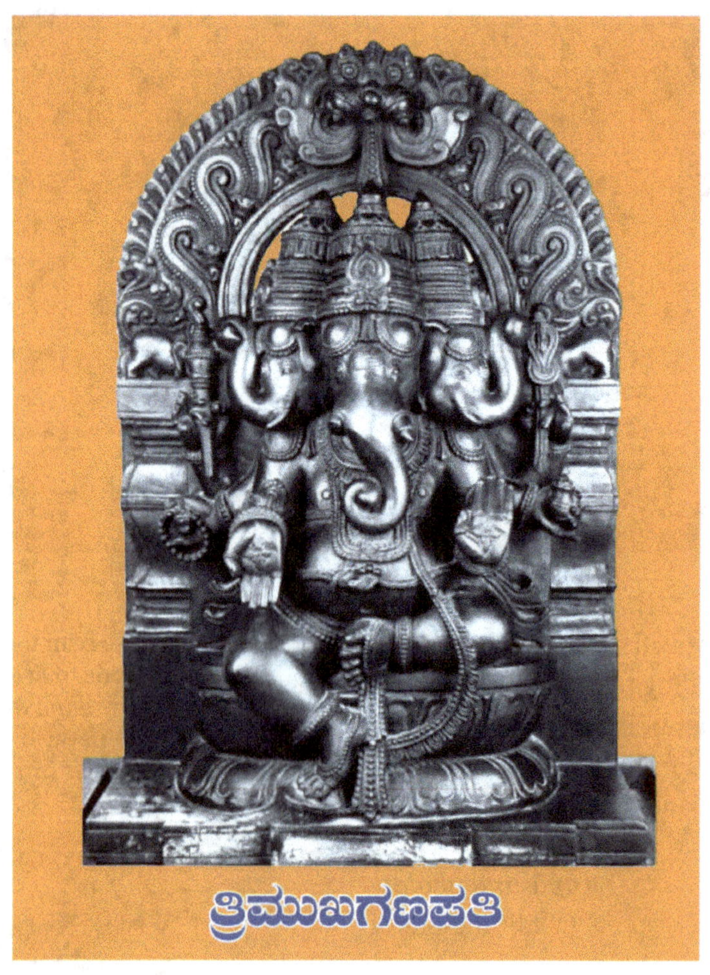

Suggested for those with the birth *nakshatra*
Dhaniṣṭā (धनिष्ठा)

28. ಶ್ರೀ ತ್ರಿಮುಖ ಗಣಪತಿ (Śrī Trimukha Gaṇapati)

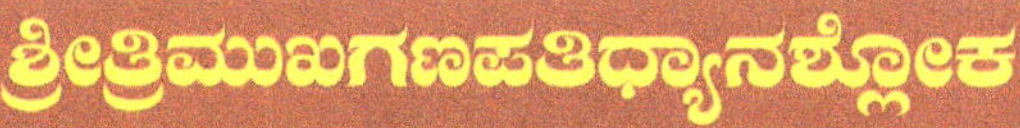

Śrī Trimukha Gaṇapati dhyāna śloka

May *Trimukha Gaṇapati* with heads shining like a *palāsh* flower having in His right hands a sharp hook and rosary and holding the (third) right hand in the boon-giving gesture, and having in His left hand a noose and a pot of nectar, and Who is seated in a golden lotus, protect us

upāsana phala:
Grace of Dattātrēya

Please scan this QR Code to listen to the *dhyāna śloka* in various languages of 🇮🇳

ॐ *Swānanda*

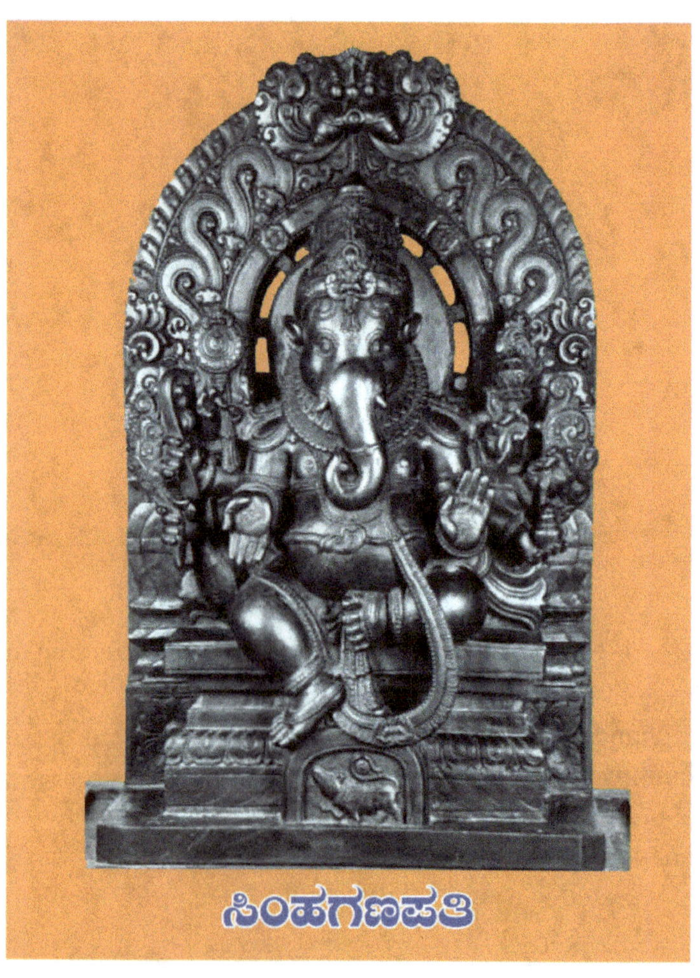

Suggested for those with the birth *nakshatra*
Śatabhiṣa (शतभिष)

29. ಶ್ರೀ ಸಿಂಹ ಗಣಪತಿ (Śrī Simha Gaṇapati)

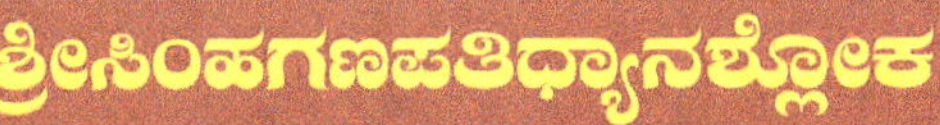

Śrī Simha Gaṇapati dhyāna śloka

May Lord *Simha Gaṇapati* adorning veena,
wish-yielding creeper, sword, and boon-giving
gesture in His right hands, and bejeweled pot,
flower bunch, and protecting gesture in His
left hands, with the trunk as fair as a conch,
and Who shines like the soft moon, and
decked with effulgent jewels, protect us from
all dangers and adversities

upāṣana phala:
Destruction of Bad Qualities

Please scan this
QR Code to listen
to the *dhyāna
śloka* in various
languages of 🇮🇳

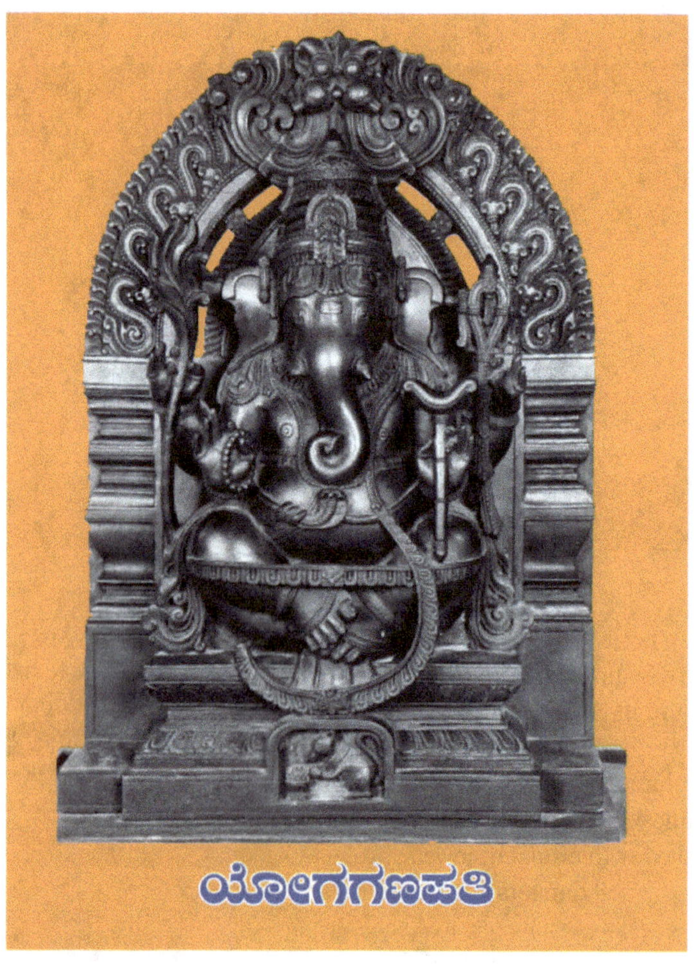

Suggested for those with the birth *nakshatra*
Pūrva Bhādrapadā (पूर्व भाद्रपदा)

30. ಶ್ರೀ ಯೋಗ ಗಣಪತಿ (Śrī Yōga Gaṇapati)

https://flic.kr/p/89rDnK

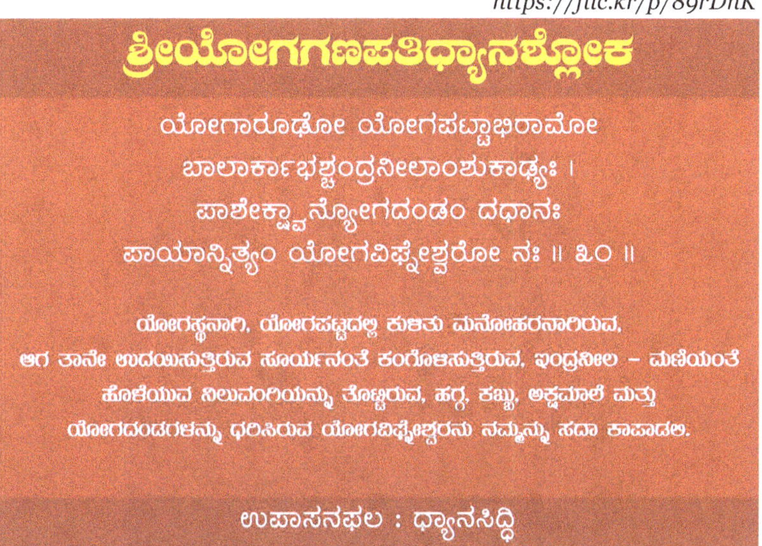

Śrī Yōga Gaṇapati dhyāna śloka

May *Yōga Gaṇapati* seated in yoga posture, in blissful meditation, radiant like the rising sun, clad in blue clothes, glowing like the soft moon, holding in His hands noose, sugarcane, arrow, and the *Yogadaṇḍa*, protect us at all times from all obstacles

upāsana phala:
Power of Meditation

Please scan this QR Code to listen to the *dhyāna śloka* in various languages of 🇮🇳

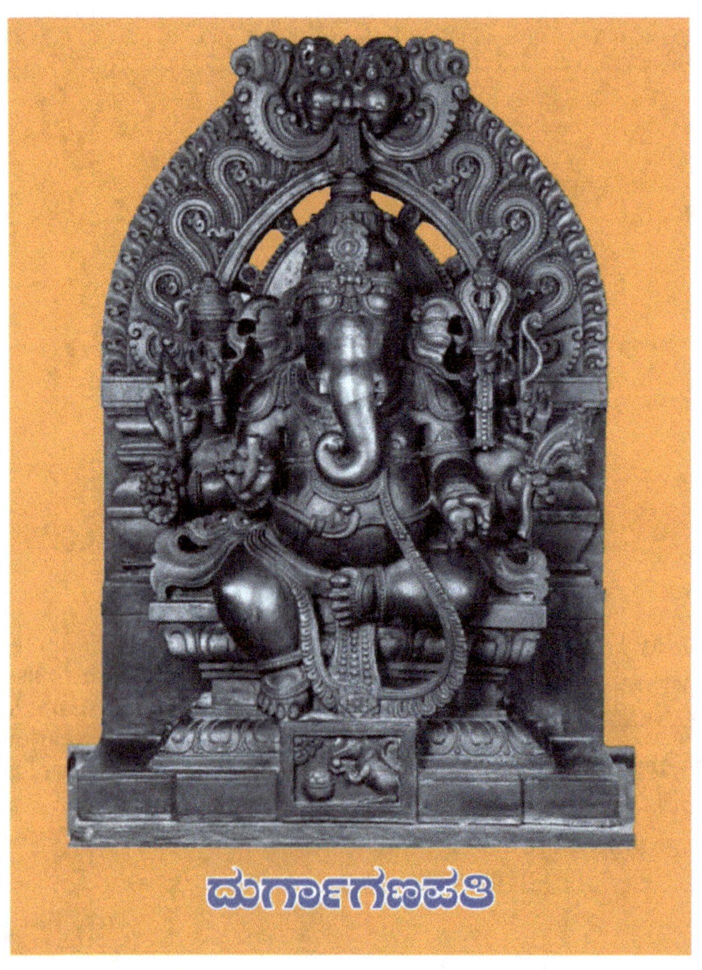

Suggested for those with the birth *nakshatra*
Uttara Bhādrapadā (उत्तर भाद्रपदा)

31. ಶ್ರೀ ದುರ್ಗಾ ಗಣಪತಿ (Śrī Durgā Gaṇapati)

https://flic.kr/p/89uU4L

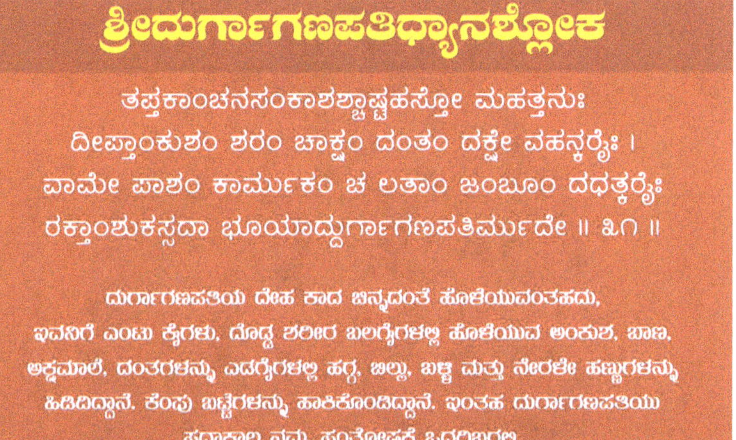

Śrī Durgā Gaṇapati dhyāna śloka

May *Durgā Gaṇapati* shining like burnished gold with a hefty body, with eight hands carrying hook, arrow, tusk, and bow in the right hands, and noose, spear, creeper, and rose apple in the left hands, and adorned with red garments, be the source of our joy and happiness

upāsana phala:
Protection during Travel

ॐ *Swānanda*

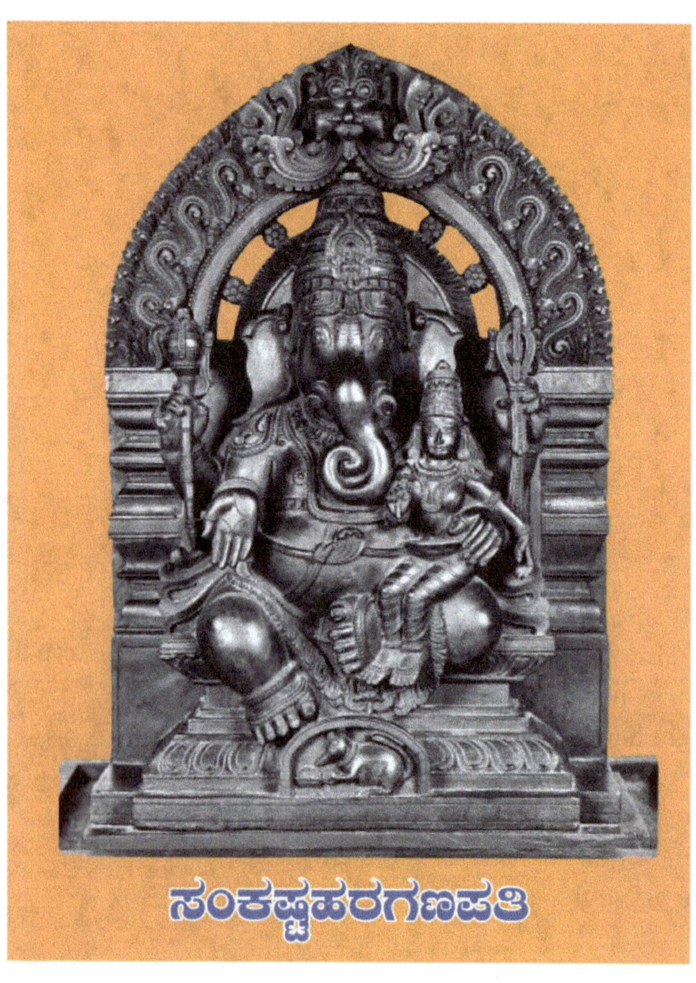

Suggested for those with the birth *nakshatra*
Revatī (रेवती)

32. ಶ್ರೀ ಸಂಕಟಹರ ಗಣಪತಿ (Śrī Saṇkaṭahara Gaṇapati)

https://flic.kr/p/89uU7W

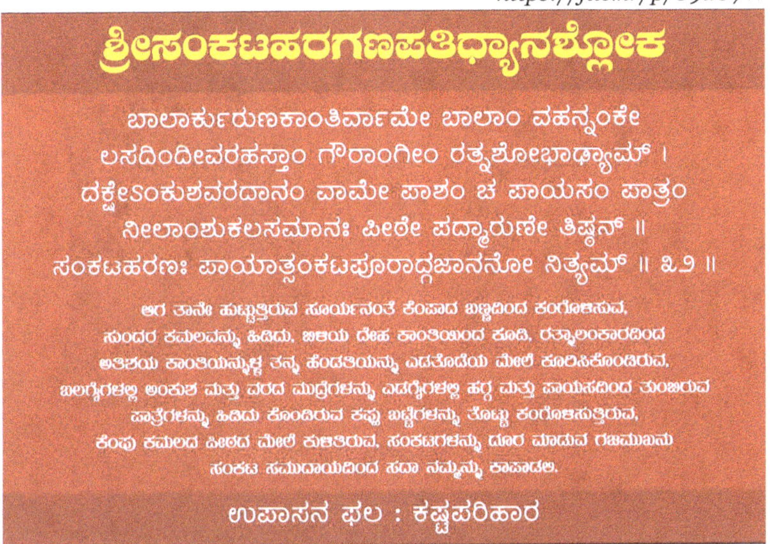

Śrī Saṇkaṭahara Gaṇapati dhyāna śloka*

May *Saṇkaṭahara Gaṇapati*, glowing like the rising sun and having lotus bearing jewel-bedecked fair goddess on His lap, adorning in His right hands hook and boon-giving gesture, and having in His hands noose and pot of *pāyasam*, seated on a red lotus, decked with blue clothes, and always engaged in removing sorrows of devotees be pleased by our *Saṇkaṭahara* worship and protect us

upāsana phala:
Solution to Difficulties

Please scan this QR Code to listen to the *dhyāna śloka* in various languages of 🇮🇳

* *Also known as* **Saṅkaṣṭahara**

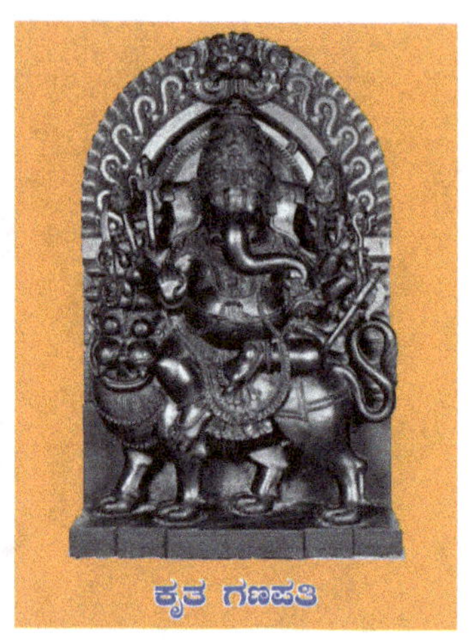

Krita Gaṇapati

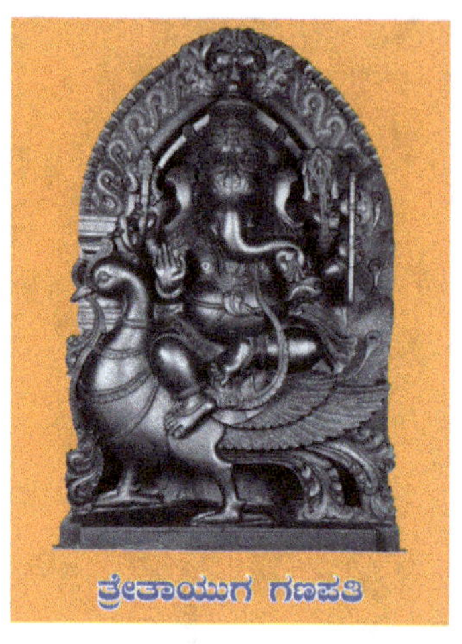

Tretāyuga Gaṇapati

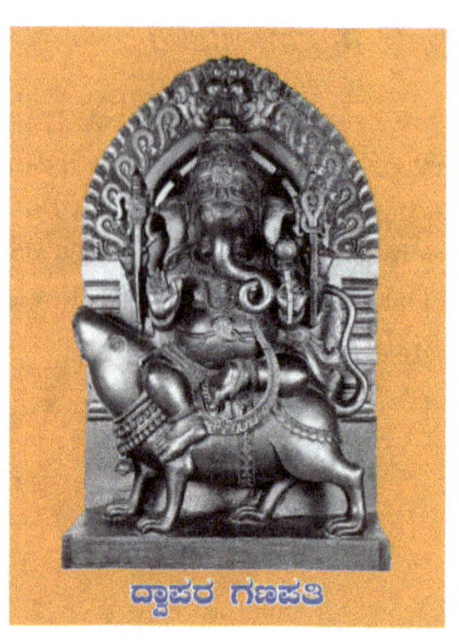

Dvāpara Gaṇapati

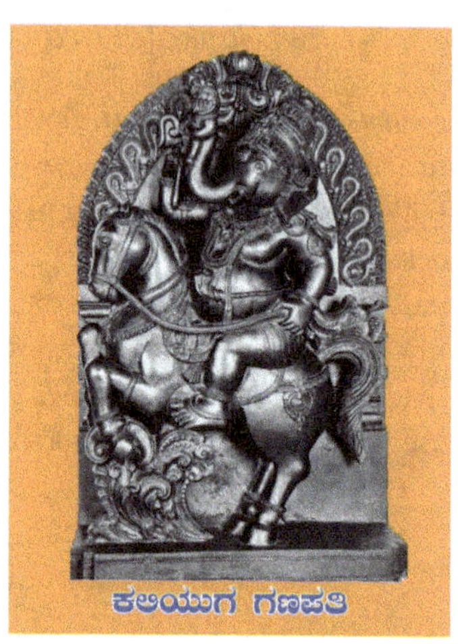

Kaliyuga Gaṇapati

ಯುಗ ಗಣಪತಿ (Yuga Gaṇapati)

In each corner of the temple complex, we find the Ganapati for
the four *yuga*

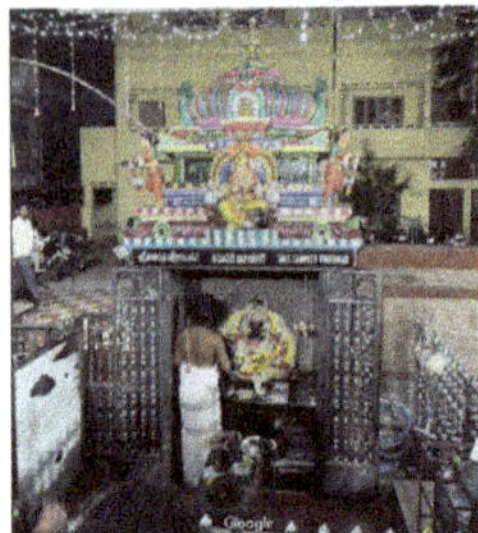

© Sravan Kumar

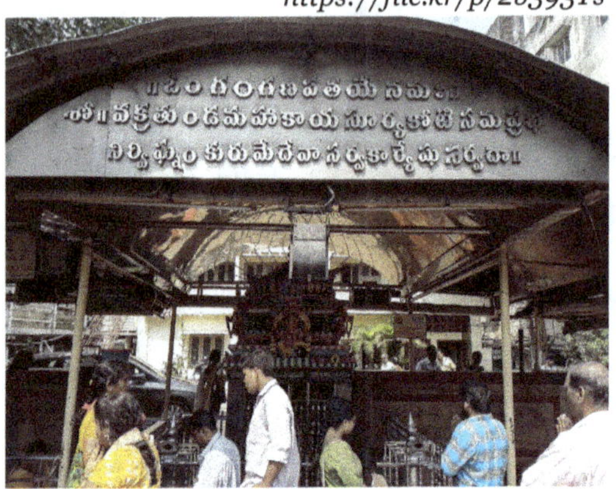

Sree Sampath Vināyagar, Vizag

Dreaming of Ganesha / Garuḍa

I have been dreaming of Ganesha of late and strongly felt that i should compile this book

The rationality bit is switched OFF in dreams. Dreams can't be understood, they can only be experienced. Just like Life

Lambōdara Vināyaka

Thursday 26th May 2022

A strange and beautiful dream this morning that filled me with a lot of exhilaration

I was in the CBM Compound of Vizag checking out a few showrooms, one of Isha Sadhguru, when i remembered that the Sampath Vināyagar temple was just further down the road

But the temple had changed into a much bigger one, opposite the road. The Main Deity was in a long narrow room, kept on the ground but **not** installed

People were referring to Him as Lambōdara Vināyaka

A lot of Sardars were around, trying to get a glimpse of the Main Deity. Wanted to ask them what's the deal, but stopped myself, which is unusual since i don't have much shame in real life!

Some kids were playing with the Main Deity, which fell off on to the ground, but no one minded. *Bālonmatta pisāchavritti*

I tried to click a few photos but lots of people were coming in between

After a while, i left, and the humongous temple also disappeared! When i asked some people around, one guy said that the old man, the Tamilian who started this temple , keeps doing weird things! I could see him playing with some things on the ground

While exiting, suddenly remembered that i should give the usual ₹21 [Love = 21 = Truth, in Numbo Jumbo] to Ganesha

One pleasant priest said that i could do that at counter #1. When i went there, i could see a weighing scale. I got two 10s but couldn't find a one-rupee coin. One more tenner got added mysteriously, and i thought 30 was as good as 21, both digitizing to 3. I gave it, citing no purpose, and the guy at the counter marveled that no deal was being made, which made me happy as well

When i exited, the road was below the main door and i had to hold a gargoyle by the neck and swing down! Was thinking: Still fit at 57!

It was slightly complex walking back, navigating many small temples and wondering whether it's OK to walk on/around them

Just when i was about to join the main road, saw some lean crows and was thinking of feeding them with something i got from the temple, but the bag was difficult to open

Was wondering whether i had any missed calls. When i checked the mobile, it looked like a remote...

ॐ *Swānanda*

Dreaming of Sri Swami Samarth as Ganesha

Thursday 23rd February 2023

Was seated in a ginormous hall for a reading of the Shri Sai Satcharita, no doubt influenced by the same going on in spirit at our local Tripura Sai Mandir during its first-year celebrations

After some time, we were all called together by Dad. Someone came around asking whether we needed coffee before it started. One guy said he'd get ready soon after his bath but i was already ready. He said the reading might take 8 hours

In the center, was a prone figure of Sri Swami Samarth. Thought that it was a carving but it was alive and breathing! The belly was huge, like a mountain. **He was famous for holding His belly and having a great big laugh.** And up to some 'trix with Shastrix (yours truly) as well. With His Ganesha-like trunk, my favorite one hugging Lord Shiva. He was tickling me with the trunk and generally having a good time

A funny mysterious dream that made me joyous

The test of a true vision is this:
It leaves a lasting spiritual impression on the mind that
generates awareness and bliss...
~Swami Vijnanananda, direct disciple of the Master

Dreaming of the Roc

Tuesday 18th July 2023

Had a dream with a huge bird, the Roc, soon after the Wimbledon MSF

It was like the **Garuḍa** of Vishnu, monstrous

It whizzed past me and nicked me with its curved talon; can still see it so clearly

It looped back in the air and kept after me

I ran off into a marshy area but the Roc didn't give up. It got trapped in the squelchy marsh, but it extricated itself and maintained its chase

I felt that it would seize me any moment; i opened my WhatsApp and gave an audio note to my family: "A Roc, like in the Tales of Sinbad the Sailor, is after me. Not sure whether i can escape it…". For once, i could get technology to work in a dream!

But i could escape from the clutches of the Roc and observed it from a distance. It changed into a gangly man and continued the search with a loping gait…

ॐ *Swānanda*

Sri Swanandaashrama

Agara Talaguni, Bengaluru 550 082.

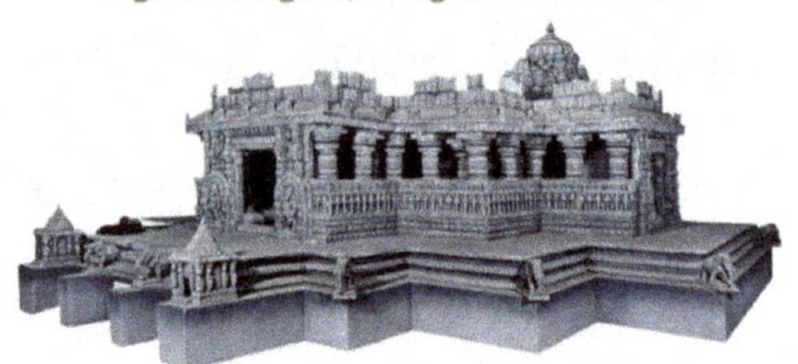

Kindly block **23** July
Sunday 2023
for **Sri Swanandaashrama**

"Swananda Milana"
is an exclusive program at Swanandaashrama

for "Expression of Gratitude n Honouring the Donors" of the shrines and well- wishers of the Ashram as per HIS Directions.

Gana Homa is being performed at the Ashram in your and your family members name.

We acknowledge your support towards **"Revival of Hoysala Architecture"** at Sri Swanandaashrama and we want to apprise you the progress of construction during your visit.

We will personally meet you to brief about the program.

Trustees
Sri Swanandaashrama

Swānanda Milānā

Very soon after the dream with the Garuḍa, we attended Swānanda Milānā on Sunday 23rd July 2023

This was a sort of a taking-stock exercise of the work done to date on the massive temple complex, as well as the way forward

It was very nice to meet the Swananda Trustees in the sylvan setting of Swānandāshrama

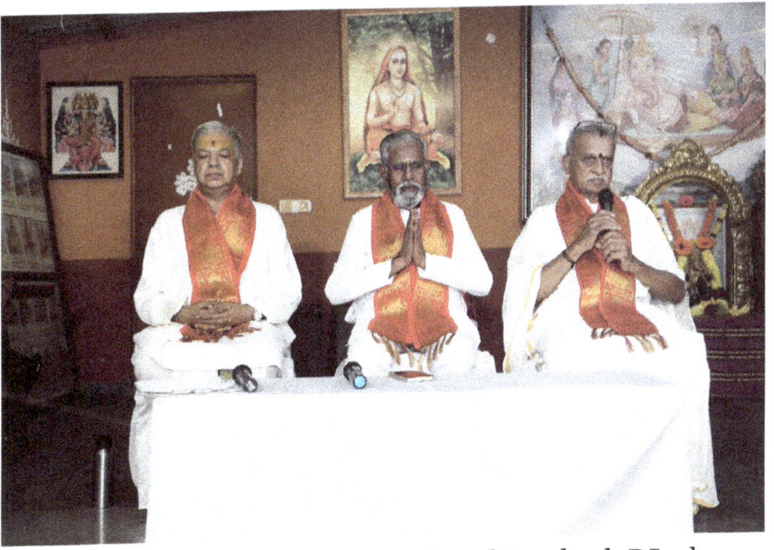

Trustees: Suresh B, BC Prasad, and Santhosh Rāvel

It was a real eye-opener to be there, to see many humble people reflecting that quote by Dame Fonteyn in their approach to life:

> The one important thing I have learned over the years is the difference between taking one's work seriously and taking one's self seriously. The first is imperative and the second is disastrous

We were also felicitated, thanks to our contribution to the Mahā Gaṇapati temple way back in 2007, which resulted in some photos that i really cherish

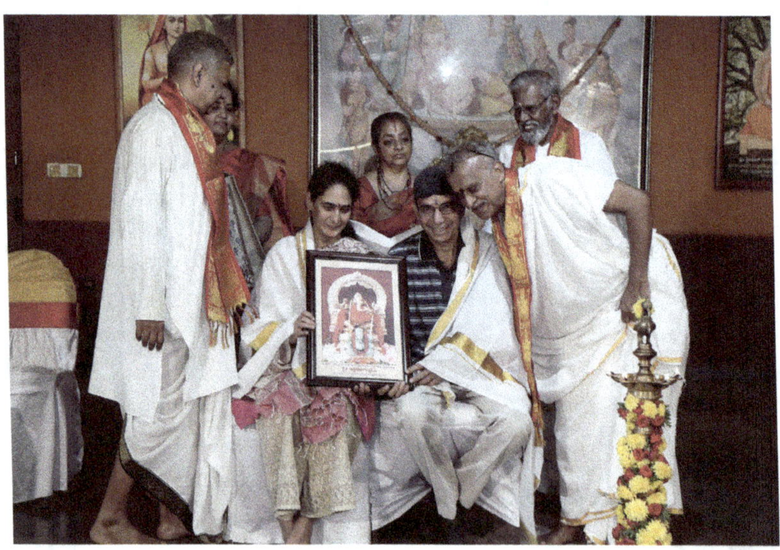

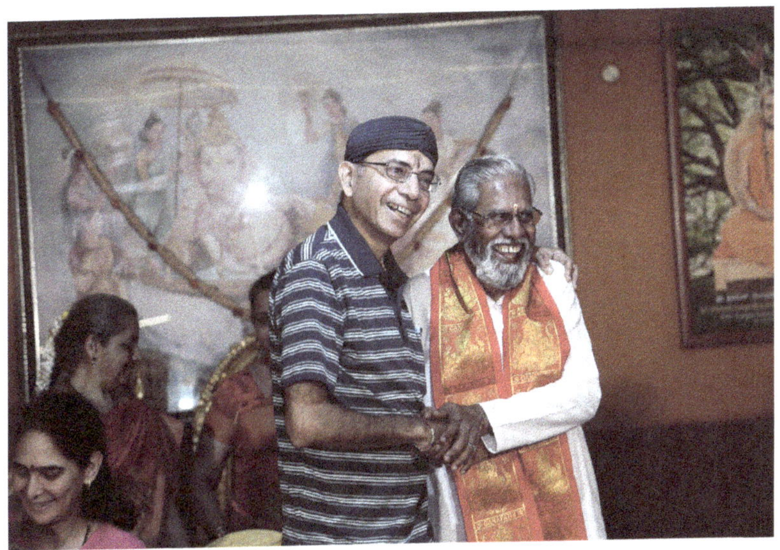

With Sri BC "We have the same birthday" Prasad

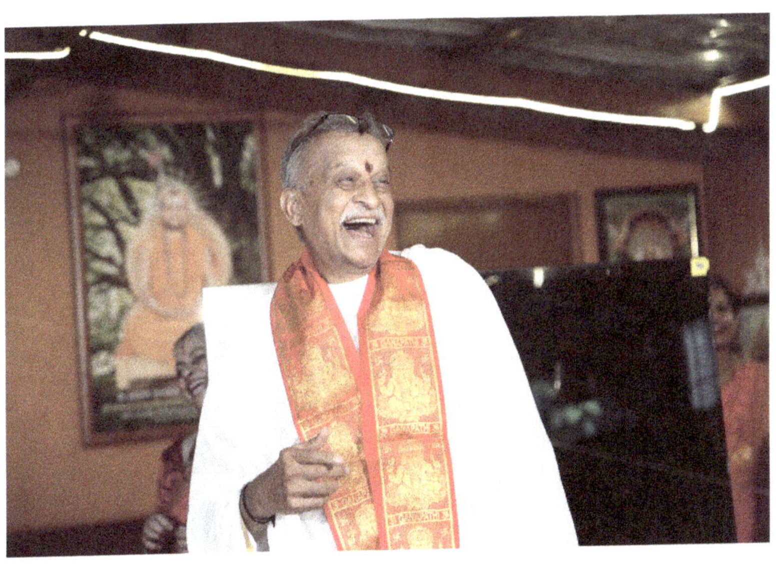

ॐ *Swānanda*

Gaṇapati pratiṣṭhāpanā mahōtsava

This book was significantly updated on the eve of *Gaṇapati pratiṣṭhāpanā mahōtsava* of Swānandāshrama temple on Thursday 18th June 2026

https://flic.kr/p/2sbog7H

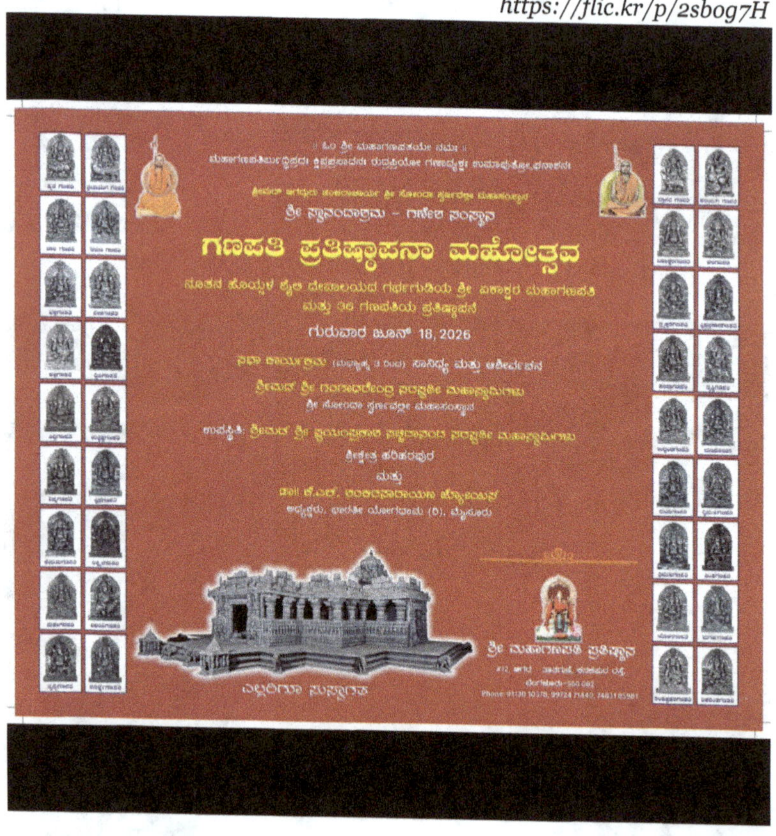

About the Author

Srinivas Shastri was born in Vizag in 1965, on the edge of Infinity, with Ramakrishna Beach separating his house on a promontory from the Bay of Bengal, the largest bay in the world

He studied Mechanical Engineering at Andhra University College of Engineering and majored in Systems and Finance at IIM, Ahmedabad in the mid~1980s

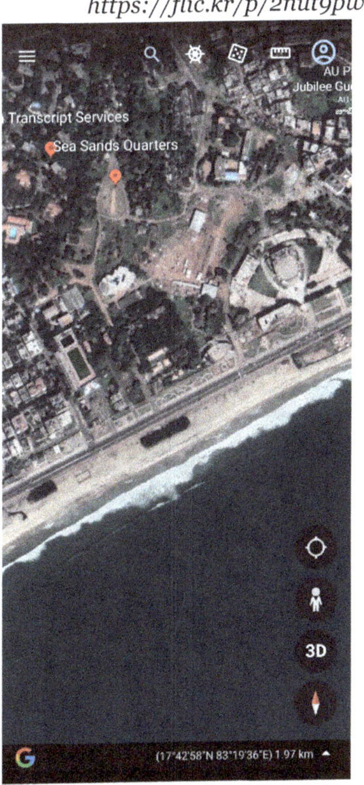

https://flic.kr/p/2nut9pw

Work was a bit of a shock for him. Somehow he did about 19 years of that, before retiring in 2006 for good. The best experience was working on the Executive Search app for Maars India, where he gleaned many nuggets about the Net, such as **asynchronous** design

This is his **ninth** book, after:

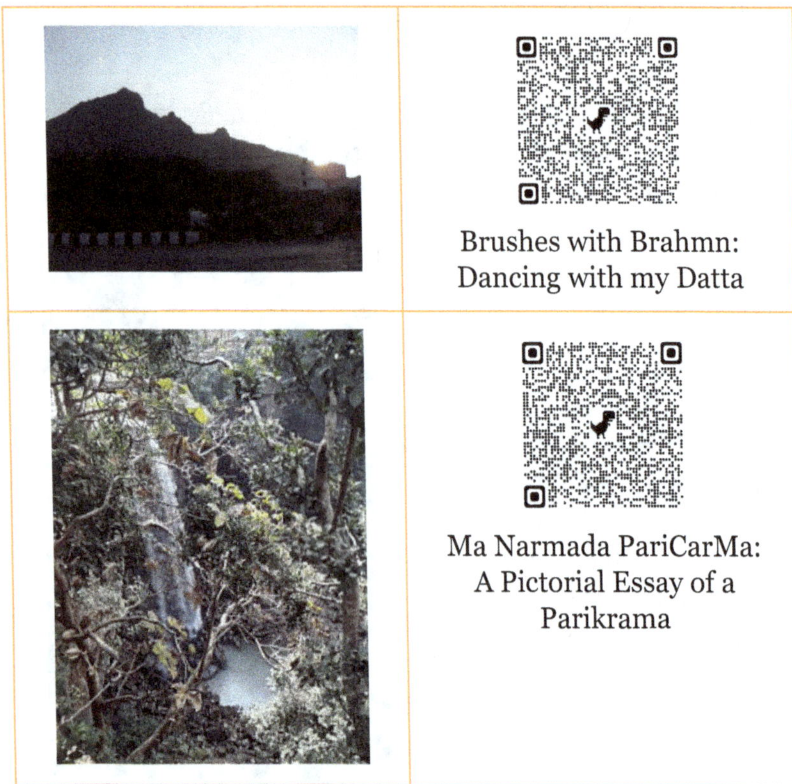

Brushes with Brahmn:
Dancing with my Datta

Ma Narmada PariCarMa:
A Pictorial Essay of a
Parikrama

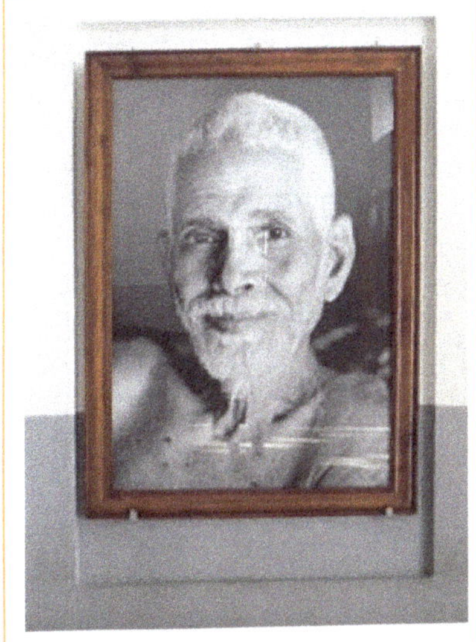

Ramanachala:
Impact of Sri Ramana
Maharshi

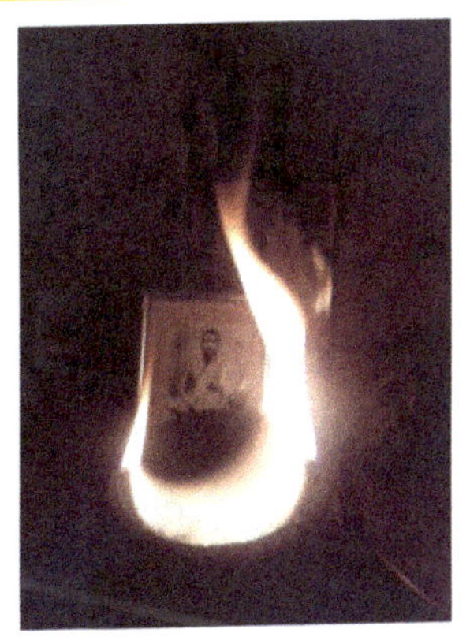

Ramakrishna:
A Maverick of a Mystic

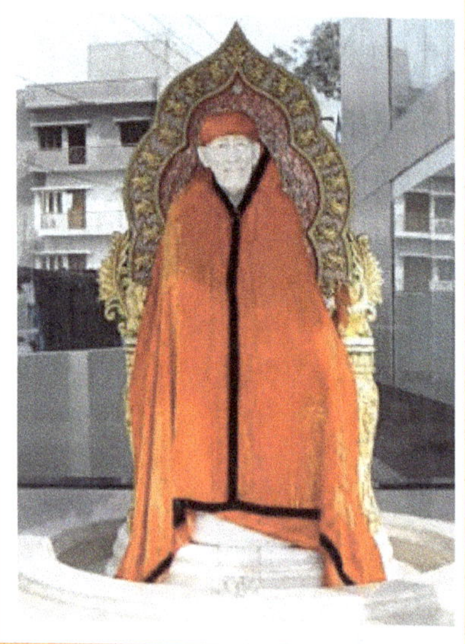

Shirdi Sai Baba:
An Akshayapātra

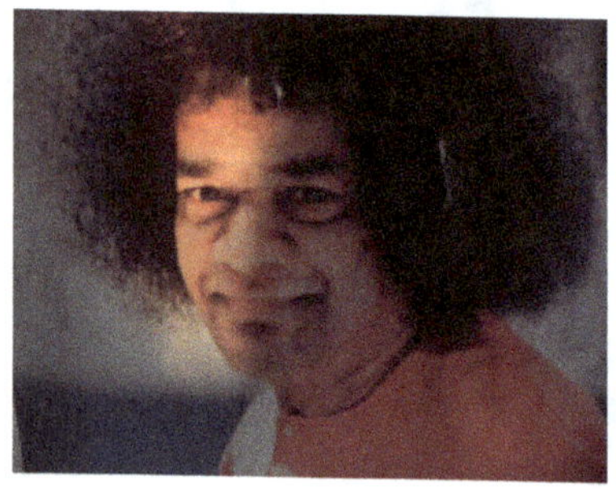

Sri Satya Sai Baba:
Love and Truth, Inc.

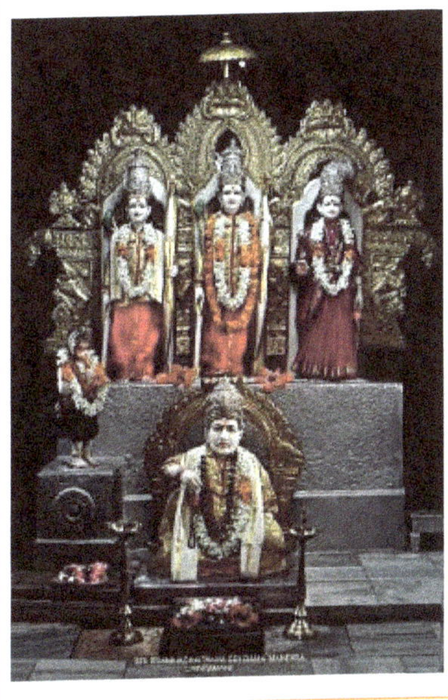

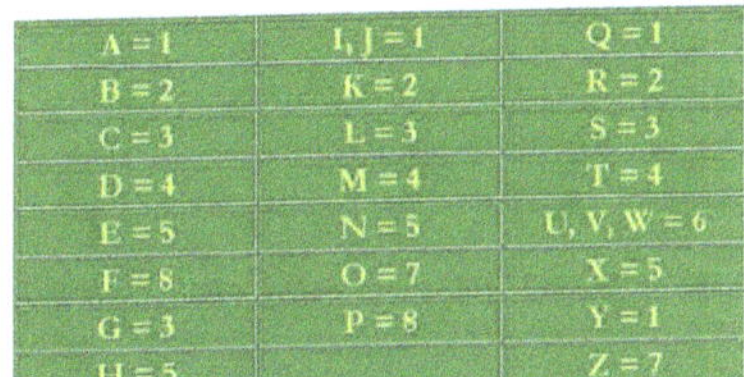

Brahmachaitanya:
Gondavalekar Maharaj

Numbo Jumbo:
My Experiments with
Numerology